mine
until

my journey into
and out of the arms
of an abuser

jessica yaffa

and dave franco

For information about this title or to order other books and/or electronic media, contact the publisher:

NoSilenceNoViolence.Inc

www.nosilencenoviolence.org

jessica@jessicayaffa.org

ISBN: 978-0-9889697-1-1

Printed in the United States of America

Cover design by: Ben Monson
Interior design by: 1106 Design

To anyone who has felt their worth taken away from them by another human being. May you draw strength from this account of my life and join me in the effort to bring an end to domestic abuse.

INTRODUCTION

MY COWRITER SAT THERE and looked at me rather windblown. I had just told him my story, never sparing a detail. He couldn't believe that this was how I wanted it to be portrayed, holding nothing back, making no attempt at self-preservation or tiptoeing around anybody's feelings. I wanted to speak about my life exactly how I remembered it—the good, the bad, and the horrific.

When he sent early drafts back to me, he had smoothed over the language and actions of the story to be a little less offensive. He asked me to consider it as it might help broaden our audience and opportunities for publishing. I could understand his point of view.

However, when I read the cleaned-up version, it actually turned my stomach a notch. It wasn't bad. It just wasn't my story. I had made a promise to the women in my ministry that I would always swing the doors of my life wide open, and I saw no reason that a book about my life should be any different.

Because of this, I want to alert my readers that this account is not G rated. The events and language are real. This book is harsh, violent and sometimes painful to read. But what you are about to experience is my life, for better or worse.

TABLE OF CONTENTS

1	Enter Sam	3
2	Message in a Paper Airplane	15
3	Love Screams	19
4	The Front	25
5	The Real Deal, Little Boy	39
6	The Trash-Covered Couch	43
7	East and West	47
8	Melanomas and Anacondas	55
9	Daydream in the Chapel	67
10	Demons in the Cathedral	75
11	Nibbling at the Heels	89
12	To the End of the Mall	95
13	The Best Place for a Murder	105
14	The Sound of the Blind	113
15	Cheap Closet Door	121
16	Splintered Wood	127

17 Exchange Gone Wrong   137
18 Park and Puke   143
19 The Slow Creep of Normalcy   153
20 Endless Hug   161
21 Payment   167
22 The Naked Doll   171
23 Whispers for the Prima Donna   179
24 Empty Girl   187
25 The Mentor Brings a Waterfall   193
26 It Means Daddy   207
27 A Societal Nerve   213
28 Peggy, Rhonda and the Power Thought   217
29 Flinch, Turn, Run   225
30 356 Front Street   231
31 When Gravity Went Missing   235
32 Little Jessica   241
Epilogue   243

In a blur, his hand moved toward my head, fingers spread apart. His palm collided with the back of my skull as his fingers clinched and created a fist full of locks. My hair pulled from my skin along my forehead and all around the crown on down to the nape of my neck. He pulled so hard my head snapped back, forcing my jaw straight to the sky, my eyes and mouth pulled as wide as they could go. My back arched sharply and painfully. His other arm hit and gripped me tightly around my torso just beneath my breasts, pushing the air from my lungs. A sound came from my mouth with no words, like an ugly, guttural squeal. He put his nose to my cheek as he breathed against my skin. Like an animal, he smelled me.

1

ENTER SAM

IT WAS 4:45 P.M. I was sitting in my car in a parking lot I felt rather lucky to have made it to. The fog that can sock in coastal San Diego is rare, but when it hits, it can be as thick as smoke.

Dusk had arrived, so there was still faint light, but I worried that in one hour when I returned to my car, I'd never be able to make it back onto the road. As I looked to the streets, I could see that there were plenty of cars zooming around as if they were trying to make it home before nightfall and visibility would drop to about 20 feet. I probably shouldn't have been out on a night like this. But with everything that was going on inside my head and heart, there was no way I was going to miss this opportunity.

I stepped out of my car into the fog and with rather unsteady legs, began my nervous walk to 365 Front Street, a one-story building whose edges were only slightly visible from a mere 30 yards away. Suite J was along the narrow courtyard that offered curvy wooden benches and a koi pond. A few of the business owners at 365 Front were stepping out and locking up, no doubt in a hurry to get home before getting stuck.

Arriving at suite J, the placard on the door read, *Anne Thompson, Marriage and Family Therapist.* I stared at it for a moment. It seemed strangely simple and inadequate. My waters ran deep, South Pacific deep. Still, Anne's website seemed to indicate expertise in the areas my life needed addressing, and I had a good feeling about this. I guess that could have just been hope.

I opened the door and found a quiet and empty waiting room and took the first seat next to the door. I noticed that there were no sounds coming from the door on the opposite end. If there was someone in there, they sure were talking softly. I leaned forward. I would expect to hear a bit of muffled talk at the very least. But it was perfectly silent.

It was almost 5 o'clock, and I expected that Anne would pop her head out any moment. I knew I had to be efficient with our time together. She ends her day at 5 p.m. and made an exception for me because I told her that my panic attacks had reached emergency level. I was hoping that there would be some way that I could get right to the problem so she could get right to the solution. It was going to be like walking a tightrope. I knew I had crater-sized issues to deal with, but there would be no way to get to them if she asked me to go too far back in my past. I was going to have to be light on my feet.

Suddenly the door opened and Anne, a tall woman with stick-straight posture and long, curly brown hair, stood just inside her office with the door knob in hand. A young, blond woman with a rumpled sweater and puffy eyes walked out, and Anne wordlessly ushered her to the door right next to where I was sitting. I was totally in the way. "I'll see you in a week," Anne said, more like a promise than a fact. "Call if you need me. Please be careful out there."

The young lady walked into the fog and Anne gently closed the door. "You must be Jessica," she said.

I stood. "Yes, hello."

"Come on in," she said with calm and composure.

Her office was less like a therapist's office than I expected, although I don't know what I expected. It was pretty and light, like a Spanish beach villa.

"So you are having panic attacks, is that right?" she asked.

"Yes, well, sort of," I said, on the spot a little quicker than I had anticipated. "It's like one big, long panic attack, I think. I mean, I hope. I mean, I hope it's just a panic attack, albeit a really long one, and it's nothing more serious, like I'm losing it or something. I'm really just hoping that if it is just one really long panic attack that you can just tell me how I can maneuver around it, and then I can come back later and really deal with it. You know, so I can get beyond it—for now." I took a deep breath.

"I see."

"But first of all, I just want to thank you again for taking me on such short notice. I'm sure you've got plenty of things to do tonight and, well, I just really appreciate it."

She motioned for me to sit down on the leather couch and then sat in a blue-and-white seat across from me. "No problem. I'm glad you're here."

"I hate that you'll have to drive in this after it gets totally dark," I told her motioning to the outside. "We can go as quickly as you want."

"No rush, I have time. I live in the condos right around the corner. But even then I'll have to watch my step. Look at it come in," she said as we both looked out the window.

I thought to myself, *Well, that didn't work.*

"Why don't we begin by you telling me a little about yourself?" I had been asked that question on many occasions for different reasons. A little always leads to a lot, it seemed, more than most people want to know or more than there is time for. Or, it is more than some people can take. I had to try to skirt around the edges so she wouldn't ask for too much, or she'd never have time to tell me what she thought I needed to do about my state of mind.

"Well," I said, taking another deep breath, "I'm going to get married really soon, as I mentioned on the phone, and I feel that if we do get married, that if he finds out, you know, what's there, and all, if I don't do a good job of, kind of, keeping it all together, and things come out and I start to act a certain way that he didn't expect, well then maybe, you know, he might not like it and I'll be a disappointment. You know what I mean?"

She looked at me quizzically for a moment. "Well, *what's there?*" she asked.

I looked at her for a second or two, trying to figure out how I might dodge what was sure to come. I couldn't come up with anything.

"Well, a lot," I answered. "There's a lot."

"Tell me about it."

"Well, okay." I hesitated. "How far back do you want me to go?"

"You know the story, not me," she said with a shrug and a smile. "Look, you're getting married, right? Let's start with your dad."

A chill went through my body. *Uh, oh,* I thought. *Here we go.*

∞∞∞∞

I don't know why his handsomeness should have had anything to do with it, but my dad's beautiful smile opened up to me like a delicately wrapped gift opens up on Valentine's Day. Perhaps it was because he was the first man to hold me in his arms and look into my eyes. But there was nothing in this world more thrilling to me, a little crazy-haired Jewish girl with hazel eyes, than when his handsome smile spread across his face—teeth dazzling, eyes aglow—and the reason for his smile was me.

My dad was tall, his shoulders were broad, and he'd wear suits to work. I loved it when he came home and popped out of the car. His ties, resting just beneath his dashing beard, were always cinched to the top, not like other dads, who would have theirs sagging low with their collars undone. Dad always looked mighty sharp. He knew it, too. Once my mom told me to tell him that he looked like a million bucks. "A million and a half," he said with a smile and wink.

My dad and I did the usual things. With my everyday outfit consisting of a blue robe, my pink tutu and slippers on the wrong feet, I rode my red tricycle down the sidewalks of our Los Angeles neighborhood under dad's watchful eye and just ahead of his playful whistle. I would talk to him without end while I rode. I'd talk about my dollies or my toys or whatever. I didn't matter. I'm sure he didn't know what I was going on about. But that was okay. I just liked to talk to him. When he called me his chatterbox, I was *his* chatterbox. It made me want to talk even more.

When we were together in the house, we would dance with my feet on his while holding hands. "1-2-3, 1-2-3," he'd say. "Hey look, honey, Jessica's already a fantastic waltzer! How could she know something like that?" He would act like he was dead with his tongue out, then alive, every time I touched him with my magic wand. He would carry me on his shoulders and I would hold on by wrapping my hands around his brow. Then I'd slide my hands over his eyes and he'd scream and do the mummy walk. "What's going on here!" he'd joke. I loved it when he joked. Once when my mom had to be away for two months, we ate nothing but pizza and scrambled eggs the entire time. I didn't mind at all. He acted like we were getting away with murder because mom wasn't there to stop us. It was "our little secret." He liked to tell me that when I was a baby, he was the only one who could get me to eat or stop fussing. When I was crying, he would plop me over his shoulder like his "little sack of potatoes" and bounce me around the house. I loved when he talked about when I was a baby.

Dad was always in my head in one way or another. He was constantly singing Paul Simon's *Kodachrome*, or *Still Crazy After All These Years* or Bonnie Raitt's *Angel From Montgomery*. Mom would roll her eyes, give a chuckle and say that daddy's lousy singing hurt her ears. It didn't hurt mine. I thought he sounded great. During the winter months, dad's joy and disgust echoed around the halls as he lived and died with the Lakers and the UCLA Bruins basketball team. My dad loved them. Of course, I did, too.

When I was about five, I would increasingly find my dad at the dining table after dinner with lots of books stacked around him. I was not to go in the dining room when he was reading those books, and when I did, he would shoo me away and tell me to be quiet.

As time went by, my dad was at the dining room table more and more, and some nights he never left. Sometimes on weekends, a whole day and night would pass and I barely saw him at all. Even when he was at work and wasn't sitting at the dining room table, I'd have a feeling of anger just to walk past it and see all those books stacked up against the wall.

I'd ask him to play. Sometimes he would do it. But the time he could spend with me was very short. He'd let me put my boas and necklaces on him. Or he'd sit at my little table and let me serve him tea or pretend bread. But he always seemed to be thinking about something else. It's hard to play characters when your mind is thinking about something else.

Sometimes I would be over at my friends' houses when their dads came home and it was usually like a party had broken out. They would pull off their shirts and throw us into the blow-up pool and shoot us with the hose. Or we'd go down the way to the park and they'd do double duty pushing us on the swings, or act like a bear outside the playhouse and we'd scream ourselves silly.

My dad didn't do that. As the years passed, he and his beautiful smile appeared less and less, and even for a very young girl, I knew deep inside that something wasn't quite right.

Was it me?

Now, I'm not the first little girl to have a distant dad, and I won't be the last. But I just might have been the most tenacious. It ignited in me a relentless desire to win my dad's affection and approval, and soon it became the only thing I thought about. Because when I saw my dad's smile, I was a good girl. But when I didn't, I knew he was unhappy with me. And I guess the ache in my heart told my brain I couldn't live that way.

I would spend much of my days strategizing about what I was going to do when he got home from work. Ask him to play? Get him his slippers? Wear a pretty dress? Greet him at the car with something to drink? Tell him a lie about how well I did in Hebrew school?

Yet, for all the passion I was feeling about becoming the object of my dad's attention, it was nothing compared to the panic that was to come. When I was six years old, Sam, my baby brother, was born.

My dad didn't just love Sam. From the time Sam arrived, my dad was absolutely head-over-hills smitten with him. He held and smiled and sang to and smothered Sam with kisses and played with his new little boy with unbridled joy and laughter. All of it happened as if no one else was in the room. But I was in the room.

It didn't matter that he talked to me or tucked me in at night or picked me up for this or that reason. When he looked at me, it was one thing. When he looked at Sam, it was something entirely different. I could feel my own invisibility.

I was suddenly transformed into a little girl dangling along the side of a cliff, holding on to a rope and trying to pull herself up with all her might. I felt the exhaustion that comes with climbing and never getting anywhere. I would think to myself, *Why does dad not love me? What is wrong with me? I have to get dad to love me. I want to be in his arms. I want him to toss me up. Why only Sam?*

As Sam grew older, it got worse. Sam was bright beyond brilliant, cute, good-natured and rarely a problem. His sharp mind was the source of my dad's delight. I was the source of my dad's frustration. I wasn't smart. I didn't get good grades. I didn't get stuff when he explained it. I wasn't pretty. I wasn't athletic. I always brought home high drama because of something one of my girlfriends inevitably would say to me to hurt my feelings and that kind of sensitivity infuriated my dad. Plus I asked, *Why?* more times than he could answer, *Because I said so.*

Actually, he never told me I wasn't cute enough, but I knew it was true. The kids at school told me that I had a nose that was too big, hair that was too curly and legs that were too skinny. It hurt terribly. I hated being Jewish and having a stupid last name. I would walk in the house after school feeling that I was a hideous loser. There was no way my dad could have thought I was pretty. He certainly never said it without me begging for it.

Every time I put on a dress, I asked my dad if he thought it was pretty. He would always say it was. The problem was in how he said it. "Yes," he'd say. "Boy, that sure is pretty." When Sam put on a baseball uniform, however, he nearly hit the roof with excitement. He would say Sam looked like an all-pro blahbitty blah and start lifting him up. What made it worse was that Sam never even had to ask.

There were plenty of times I would ask my dad to play with me and he would say he was too busy, only to find him playing with Sam just minutes later. Sam wanted to talk about America and George Washington and Thomas Jefferson and my dad couldn't have been happier to oblige him. Sam and my dad would read the encyclopedia together, and my dad beamed over his smart boy. When Sam announced he wanted to be the president of the United States, dad almost fell out of his chair. I couldn't compete with that.

In the meantime, I was awful to Sam. I threw my skates into his face. In Hawaii, I ran him face-first into a tree. When we moved to San Diego when I was in the sixth grade, I would tell him that the lady across the street in our new San Diego neighborhood was a kidnapper and that as soon as he would walk into the front yard, she was going to take him. In fact, I wished she would take him. He freaked out. It was perfect.

For all my efforts, nothing seemed to make my dad warm up to me. He was mine until Sam came along. Now, he seemed to get more distant with each passing day, as if all my trying was making things worse. What was I to do, let him drift away?

By now he was a busy lawyer, travelling multiple days of each week. When he would call my mom at night, I couldn't wait to get on the phone and tell him about my day and that I loved him. He would tell me he loved me, too. I guess I believed he meant it. But that wasn't really the point. I wanted him to make me feel like he loved me as much as he loved Sam—that I had made it to the deepest part of his heart. But it never happened, not even close.

When I was 15, my parents took Sam and me to Rome. I was excited to go as I had heard that the nightlife in Rome was spectacular. Now, there's only so much nightlife a 15-year-old girl can experience, but I had romanticized it so much in my head that I just had to see it.

Each day my mom and dad dragged me and Sam through every museum in the city, and by the time the day was over, they were exhausted. Each night we stayed in and played cards or read or watched Italian TV. On one of the last nights, after days of begging my dad to take us out for an evening, he finally said yes. I was so excited I counted the minutes. We spent the day in yet another dreary museum, but it didn't matter. I was finally going to see Rome at night.

When we got to the hotel late that afternoon, my dad was bushed. I saw him yawning. I got ready as fast as I could so I would force his hand in case he had any ideas about cancelling our evening. I was simply putting on my dress and brushing my hair, but in my own way, I was fighting for survival. My dad didn't give in to my wishes very often, and now that I owned this one, it was going to happen no matter what.

When he ultimately did tell me he was too tired to take us out, even I was surprised at what happened next. Right there in the middle of our hotel room I managed to pull off one of the great meltdowns in Roman history. I lay on the floor and cried and screamed like a four-year-old little girl in a department store who had fallen in love with a doll that her mother would not buy. My dad was emotionally wrecked by the incident, and I completely ruined his and everybody else's night. I guess that's what you get when you ignore your daughter for 15 years.

If being a little Jewish girl with a big nose, out-of-control hair and skinny legs was tough, it was a joyride compared to being an adolescent with all the same features. I desperately wanted to get the attention of boys, and as hard as I looked for any sign of it, I rarely saw any. I joined the swim team to be in my bathing suit near the boy swimmers, and while I did receive a few looks, it was nothing when I saw what the other girls were getting. When my teammates, some I considered friends, would comment on my odd looks, it was particularly devastating. I got *this* close to getting them together and actually laying it all out and pleading with them to be nice to me. Home had become completely unsafe ground—my friends simply *had* to be nice. If they weren't, I had nowhere to turn. In the meantime, if they had any need whatsoever, I was there. I became a *care* junkie. Living life as an open wound as I did, all injury was deeply meaningful to me. If my friends experienced any pain at all, whether from boys or school or parents or each other, I was able to enter into their hurt, encourage them, tell them why they were special and offer a shoulder to cry on. I wasn't afraid of tears. I knew my way around tears.

I remember walking up and down the halls of my high school feeling exhausted. I felt like I had been chasing after the wind my entire life. I wanted to stop the churning that was going on inside. Even so, my default position was to pursue my dad's love, and I couldn't turn it off. I was still so obsessed with him that even though my mom was right alongside me every day, I barely remember a thing about her.

The sun was shining brightly the morning of the first day of my last semester as a senior. I looked out my bedroom window and recognized the false brilliance of January sunrays in San Diego. They only look warm. I dragged myself out of bed, got ready and arrived at school a bit early to verify with the office that the schedule and class change that I had requested had been approved. It had. I was transferring over to Mrs. Clift's class, whom I had had before and knew that she was an easy A. In fact, this entire semester was going to be easy. I had a light load, with archery being one of my classes. And so, with nothing particular on my mind, I walked down the corridor and into my new English class. It seemed like an odd day to also walk into my future.

∞∞∞∞

Did you play with dolls?
Oh yeah, all the time.
What did they say?
The dolls?
When you made conversation between the dolls?
Oh. Well I had two doll phases. One with my baby dolls and then another with my Barbies. Actually, Ken did most of the talking to Barbie. He was always telling her how beautiful she was and that she was the perfect princess he would do anything for. I really loved the whole princess scenario, where she would be saved by Ken who would come crashing in and risk life and limb.
I bet those were exciting times.
Yes, they were, as a matter of fact.
And your babies?
My babies didn't talk. I just talked as the mom to them.
What did you say to them?
That they were perfect just the way they were.

2

MESSAGE IN A PAPER AIRPLANE

"JESSICA YAFFA?" Mrs. Clift said as she took roll call.

I raised my hand. "Here."

"Hello, Honey," Mrs. Clift replied, looking up at me. Just then a handsome black face a few rows in front of me turned to see who had the odd name. "Yaffa?" he mouthed, showing his teeth like a gopher. I gave him a *what's-with-you* look. He laughed.

That's really all it took. *Hmm*, I thought.

Trent Michaels was a star wrestler and super stud with as many muscles as can be packed onto a 5'7" frame. He had a smile that flashed like bicycle reflectors and a bad-boy gleam in his eyes. He was also the most relentless class clown I had ever seen. When Mrs. Clift would turn her back, he would silently but enthusiastically dance while seated. When she would turn around, Trent's split-second reaction would have him looking like the picture of deep thought and studiousness before she could catch him. Of course, the entire class would bust a gut trying to choke back the laughter. I was in awe of him immediately.

When it was his turn to read out loud, he would read in character. For *Beowulf,* he pulled out a dramatic English accent, low growls for men or high pitched for women. Funny thing was, he was so good at it—so believable, we couldn't wait for his turn to read. Despite her frustrations with him, I don't think Mrs. Clift could, either.

Another time, he organized a campaign of getting people across all the different rows to pick up their desks and move them toward the center of the classroom every time Mrs. Clift turned toward the black board. Student by student, inch by inch, the rows scrunched closer together until finally Mrs. Clift looked out and saw us all huddled together like a traffic jam in the middle of the room. Mrs. Clift's face went askew, as if to say, *Am I going crazy?*

Poor Mrs. Clift was no match for the force that was Trent, with all his wisecracks, impersonations and shenanigans. A few times she even threatened him with detention and extra classwork while laughing hysterically.

One day, I got a paper airplane to the side of the head. I looked around and Trent was pointing to himself. He motioned for me to open up the airplane. Inside, it read, "We have to happen." I rolled my eyes at him. I wadded up the paper as if it were trash, but kept it in my purse, flattening it later. I felt my heart begin to thump.

After class, he caught up with me in the hall, which wasn't difficult considering I was walking slowly just for that reason. "Hey, Yaffa!" he barked, running toward me.

"Yes," I said as I turned around. He stopped in front of me.

"Come here," he told me, motioning toward the lockers. He looked me over for a moment like I was dinner. "You're unbelievable, man."

I smiled at him. "What are you talking about?"

"You're the most gorgeous thing I've ever seen." I immediately felt hot all over. "What does a guy have to do to get a woman like you?" he said. He shook his head from side to side. "Mmm, mmm, mmm."

I looked down the hall in both directions as if I were doing something wrong. He never took his eyes off me.

"One thing for sure, if I had a woman like you," he said, "I'd never leave you alone."

There I was, a starving girl for 16 years, now feasting on the attention, on his words, on his gaze. I could feel my body and soul change right then and there. I was finally being nourished—drips of sweet milk rolling down my thirsty soul. I looked at my watch. I was late for my next class on the other side of school. I wrote down my number. "Call me?"

"Damn right," he said grinning like a cat outside a birdcage.

That weekend, Trent and I went on a date, and then another, and we fell in love. Before long, we were inseparable. In his arms I was all that I had never been. I was beautiful, smart, witty and interesting. When he wasn't making me crack up, he was busy lavishing me with praises and kisses. "Pretty," was his nickname for me. I loved it. He would leave love notes and cards for me everywhere, often with a single rose. I would find them at my locker, on my windshield, at my desk, in my coat pockets.

> Dear Pretty,
>> Do you know how many times I have thought about you today? Just once. But wouldn't you know it—it has lasted all day?

Trent didn't have a lot in the way of possessions. It may have been part of the reason why every time he looked at me it was as if I had just walked out of his dream, like a man stranded on a deserted island turns to find it is also inhabited by a princess. "I can't believe you're here," he would say. "I can't believe you're mine."

He did any odd job he could find, *anything*, to earn enough money to treat me right. He'd always buy me something to eat with a pocket full of change. It was adorable. He managed to take me to movies; once, he even paid for us to go to Magic Mountain and bought me everything I wanted. He was trying so hard to impress me. He succeeded, although all he had to do was dance. I couldn't get enough of it. He would break into a wacky jig that had his pelvis and shoulders and head and legs going in every direction—all with a face of conviction that this dance was the most important artistic expression in the world. I was on the floor.

One night when he came by to pick me up, he looked like he had seen a ghost. "What's the matter?" I asked him over and over. "Nothing. It's nothing," he kept saying as he drove. I tried to pull his face toward me, but he wouldn't allow it, keeping his eyes firmly on the road. He drove me to the highest point on the coast of San Diego, a small grassy area overlooking the freeway in La Jolla. We sat on a bench in the moonlight and looked down on the cars below, saying mostly nothing. He put his head on my lap and I heard him begin to sniffle.

"Oh, my God," I said. "Would you please tell me what's going on?" Trent took his time getting to an answer.

"I've seen a lot of things," Trent said in a whisper.

"What kinds of things, babe?"

"I've just seen a lot of things, Jess." He lifted his head. "Is it okay if I don't tell you what they are? Can you be okay with that?"

His eyes were filled with tears, and the left side of his face looked swollen. "Sure," I said. "As long as I know you're alright." I reached to touch his puffy cheek. He grabbed my wrist and kissed the palm of my hand, keeping his lips against it.

"I have you, now. I'm alright." He put his head back down on my lap. I thought deeply about what I had just seen as I stroked his hair. A few moments went by. "We're going to get married one day, right?" he asked.

"Of course, babe," I said. "Of course we will."

I meant every word.

3

LOVE SCREAMS

"YOU'RE A COMPLETELY DIFFERENT caliber of woman than anyone I've ever been with," he said. *Caliber of woman,* I thought. Man, that felt sexy. He wanted my body. If there was more of this feeling in sex, I absolutely wanted to give it to him.

Trent and I had sex every chance we could. It was rough and dangerous and in conspicuous places. We'd go out to get something to eat, have sex in his mom's car, then he'd take me home and we'd call each other and talk about what we had done until it was so late we ended the night whispering in our beds. It was thrilling.

He was so alive around me—always on edge, like my own personal bodyguard. After each class he would wait at my locker to escort me to my next class, always looking around and up and down the halls as if he were in the Secret Service and I were an important dignitary. Trent would say that the other boys were constantly looking at me. I didn't see it, but I sure liked him saying it.

19

He started demanding that I pick him up and drive him to school because he wanted to see me first thing in the morning. More times than not, he'd start by saying something about my tight-fitting clothes or makeup. "I'd rethink that," he'd say if my neckline was too low. Or, "I hope I don't see that again," he'd say when my pants appeared too tight. Or, on a day when I wore shiny red lip gloss, "I'd tone that down if I were you."

"He wants me to be modest," I'd say to myself. "It's probably for my own good."

He loved me so much he wanted me to call him immediately upon walking in the door after school so he could know I had "arrived safely." For my own protection, he didn't want me to go to any school parties or functions. "Protection from what?" I asked him.

"That's my business," he said. "Just leave that to me."

After school, I would hurry home and try to complete my schoolwork until he got out of practice. Then I'd have to drive back to school and pick him up. We'd usually spend the rest of the evening together. It got to be where I never saw my friends after school anymore. My only chance to see them was at school—but even that was about to change.

"I don't like your friends," he said.

"Sue and Connie?"

"All of them. They're party girls. They're bad influences."

"How?"

"They dress like skanks."

"No, they don't, and I don't think I dress like them, anyway."

"I don't care what you think. I don't want you hanging around them. We're together now," he said.

It was true that Connie and Sue and the other girls I was hanging out with were always trying to pull me away to a different party or basketball game, and that only seemed to cause trouble with Trent. I guess I could see what he was saying. If I had him, why did I need them?

Trent had managed to control my time before school, after school, between classes, break and lunch. But what he couldn't control was my time in class. It soon became a problem. He was convinced that each class was not only an opportunity for other guys to hit on me, but for me to try to lure them in as well. Our end-of-night phone conversations became entirely about "other guys." He would say, "Come on, with a woman as beautiful and sexy as you, you're trying to tell me that nobody tried to put a move on you? That's bullshit. That's just not the way things work."

I liked that he felt I was so hot that every guy would be sexually charged around me. The problem was, he could not be convinced that nothing had happened. Soon we found ourselves in nightly fights that would result in multiple hang-ups and calls back, screaming and often, tears. We had graduated from whispered, tee-hee talk about sex to full-throated blowouts about boys who never existed. They usually lasted late into the night or early the next morning.

My parents were miserable. They would sit me down and try to convince me that normal relationships didn't act that way. Suddenly my parents faced two wars: the nightly ones between Trent and I, and the ones they would find themselves in every time they tried to convince me Trent was no good. The way I saw it, my relationship with Trent was untouchable. I defended it like a rabid dog. Red in the face and exhausted, they gave up. I had showed them.

The day of the senior prom was so exciting I could hardly stand it. My single-strap, white-and-silver dress was the most beautiful thing I had ever laid eyes on. I couldn't wait to put it on and feel like I did when I had tried it on in the store—when I stood in front of the three-way mirror and pulled my hair to the top of my head. It was the first time I ever looked at myself and got a glimpse of what Trent had been seeing. I looked sexy.

I took it off the hanger, draped it over my bed and excitedly sat in front of my mom's vanity to do my makeup. I had gotten my hair to sit just so on top of my head when the phone rang.

"Hello?"

"It's Trent. We ain't going."

"What do you mean?"

"My fucking cousin says I can't have his Cadillac after all, the fuck!"

"So what—now you're not taking me?"

"You heard me. We're not going!"

He slammed the phone in my ear. I began to panic. I called him back.

"What!" he yelled.

"This is ridiculous! Take your mom's car. I don't care what car we go in!"

"That's a piece of shit. I'm not going in a piece of shit." He slammed the phone again. I ran out down the hall and found my dad and asked him if Trent could take his car. "Can he drive a stick?" he asked.

"No."

"Then he can't take my car."

My mom's car was a big sedan and in good shape. I didn't even bother asking, I just went straight to begging. "Please, mom, Trent's cousin won't let Trent take his car and he won't take me in his mom's car and dad says we can't take his so can we take yours?"

∞∞∞∞

What did she say?

She said yes.

So you went?

Yeah.

Did you have a good time?

Actually we did.

That's remarkable.

Why?

Well, you wouldn't have brought it up if it wasn't significant.

That's true.

So why was it significant enough to bring up?

Because it was so absurd.

Is that it?

What else?

You tell me?

I don't know. It was a crazy thing to do to someone.

Why?

Well, just because he couldn't get that stupid car, he was willing to kill my prom night.

Why was he willing to kill your prom night?

I don't know; I guess because he was a jerk.

It's nothing more than that?

Well...because he didn't really care about me?

So let me ask you again, what else were his actions besides absurd?

Familiar?

4

THE FRONT

SEVEN MONTHS PRIOR, when the school year began, talk of what college I would attend the following year was an exciting nightly topic of discussion around the dinner table. Now, because of my relationship with Trent, there was an increase in the intensity and seriousness with which my parents talked about it. It seemed as though they anticipated that I would soon be demanding to attend a local college, and they were going to shut down that possibility before it ever began. My dad talked with a clenched fist and tapped his finger to make his point, saying that I just had to get away to college to get the "college experience," that "getting away would help me grow up," and that there was "nothing better for a young person." It was all a lot of crap. They just wanted me to be away from Trent.

They had their reasons. Trent and I had made their lives unbearable. In addition to the nightly fighting, my trying to please Trent at all costs, the level of control that I had given up to Trent plus a drastic change to my style of dress, I gave them one more thing to come unglued about: when we went on family day-trips, which my family often did, Trent didn't like me being away from him. So he pushed me into pressuring my parents into letting him go along—and I did so without hesitation.

When I did, it was always a disaster. Still, like a cannon bolted to the concrete, I stood my ground and fired off my demands that they let him come. There was screaming, storming around, slamming doors, the works. If they ultimately agreed to letting Trent join us, we were all so war-torn from the fighting, it was usually an outing where Trent and I went off on our own while they brooded. When we were about to take a family vacation to England, I pushed for Trent to come along even then. We fought bitterly for days with neither side giving an inch. Finally, I had to accept that they would not relent, and even with Trent pushing me to continue the fight, our trip was fast approaching, and I had to give it up. I know mom and dad thought they'd won, but they hadn't. While in England, I threw a fit to be able to call Trent as much as he wanted to be called, which meant many times a day. There I would be, in a British phone booth, in a screaming match with Trent about British boys he thought I was wooing, racking up long-distance charges on my dad's bill, with my dad just a few feet away, looking like he was going to kill me the moment I stepped out. At the same time my mom would be doing her best to talk him off the cliff. Two weeks later, the moment we got home from our trip, I jumped into my car and sped away to Trent's house like a junkie in need of a fix.

Immediately, we resumed our horrible, nightly fights by phone that echoed throughout the house destroying any peace and setting everyone on edge. Trent could not be mollified or convinced that any position he held was wrong—in his mind he knew I was cheating. So each fight was like taking a horror scene out of a movie and setting it on a continuous loop. Blood-curdling screams. Crying. Frantic redialing. Many times, as we fought, he sounded like he wanted to cry—as if what we were fighting about was threatening something greater than a mere relationship with a girlfriend. I remember thinking that, for all his power and muscles, the truth was he was *this* close to falling apart at any moment.

Meanwhile, my parents and even my brother walked around hanging on by a thread. Each night, when the phone rang, everyone knew to batten down the hatches. It was going to be an awful next couple of hours.

It may have seemed to any outside observer that there was no way to elevate the level of chaos and terror in the house, but when I eventually did make my request—which turned into a demand—that I go to college in San Diego, the screaming and shrieking nearly caused the paint to peel from the walls. It was so unbearable that at one point, poor Sam was reduced to a puddle of tears in his room, hands over his ears. What made it all the more impossible was that we fought on two wavelengths, missing each other completely. My mom and dad tried to make their case with reason and logic, whereas my tactic was to simply try to make their lives miserable enough to drive them into submission. But my mom and dad fought me like this was the last hope to save their household and sanity, and they were going to hold this hill no matter the personal toll.

When I finally allowed myself to see how dug in they were, I had to figure out my next move. I came up with an idea. "I have something to tell you, Trent, and you won't like it at first, but I have a plan," I told him.

"You're not going *any-fucking-where!* That's for damn sure, Jess! I don't even want to talk about it. It's done. You're not going."

"I *am* going away," I told him. "If I don't, they won't pay for my college. Then who's going to pay for it? Me? You? It's a done deal but you don't have to worry. I've got it all figured out."

About ten minutes later, he stopped his rant long enough to listen.

"Look," I said. "One of the colleges that my dad likes is only 90 minutes away on just the other side of Orange County. I'll leave the campus right after class at 3 o'clock so that I can be at your apartment by 5 o'clock, and then I'll sleep with you. I'll schedule my classes late enough the next day so that I can drive back and be back at school in time."

Trent looked me like I was trying to sell him a bridge. He then launched into a tirade. It lasted a week. However, once he saw he could freak out all he wanted and nothing was going to change, he finally began to relent. He agreed to my offer to drive to his house after class and stay the night. But he wanted more. Much more. He wanted to have periodic "showings" at my college where we would walk around to all the public areas including the quad, outside my dorm building, inside the dorm public areas, everywhere—and we would make out. It would be a silent "announcement" to all the boys that I was unavailable.

I agreed.

I also agreed that he would have full control of when I was to be in my dorm room. If class ended at 11 o'clock, I would be in my room by 11:10 and not a minute later. I agreed to call him the moment I entered the room—no taking off my jacket, no going to the bathroom, no saying hi to my roommate. He meant *the moment*. If I didn't do it, I should expect there to be hell to pay. He also wanted me to stay in my room. "Let's not start hanging out with all those idiots," he said.

I agreed.

He also wanted periodic check-ins. I would have to call him once I got to school after leaving him in San Diego that morning and then a call during the day between classes.

I agreed.

He also demanded that my drive time from school to his apartment last only 1 hour and 40 minutes and not a minute more.

I said okay.

He also demanded that that all parties or school functions be out of consideration.

Okay.

And no matter the circumstance, there would be no talking to any boy.

I guess I could understand that. I agreed.

Even though Trent's demands were firmly in place, he still lived the months leading up to the start of school in a near state of panic. He picked a fight with me every night. They were long and nasty and exhausting.

I noticed that my mom and dad stopped poking around in my life. They quit asking questions and giving admonishments to be careful or change course. It appeared they had put all their hope on my going away to college, figuring that it would solve the things that they couldn't. They resolved to grin and bear it and steer clear of me until then.

Finally, it was the day to leave. Trent drove south to an apartment near La Mesa where he would live with members of his community college wrestling team, and I drove my packed car north to my college about 90 miles away.

Of course, I would turn around and drive back to San Diego that night. I made it to his apartment, and we argued bitterly and went to bed and had sex. The next morning I got up, had sex again, got back in my car, drove the hour and a half back to the school for my first day of college. We did this throughout the year, five out of seven nights each week, and fought by phone for the other two—always about cheating or being too available or sexy.

Although Trent came only twice to my campus for the "showings," all other agreements stayed intact. On those rare days when I didn't drive to his apartment, I figured out how to go to a friend's dorm right after class without getting into trouble with Trent. I would walk into my dorm at the designated minute, call Trent, and then forward my phone number to her apartment. At the same time that I was glad that I had bent the rules, it also reminded me that Trent had total control and total access.

Still I kept making the trips to his apartment in La Mesa, constantly gauging my speed against the time left that I had to get there.

When I saw even a hint of traffic forming on the freeway, I would curse and sweat, hitting my fists against the steering wheel. When I would arrive, I would ring his doorbell and he would open the door, look at his watch and then wordlessly walk to my car to check my mileage. If he saw more miles than he figured were needed to get to his place, he would launch into aggressive questioning about where else I had driven. On the rare occasions that I would get to the apartment before he did, he would arrive and put his hand against the car hood to gauge how hot it was. If it was too hot, he'd know that I had only just gotten there and missed my time. And there would be hell to pay.

There would be some days that I simply didn't have the energy to make the trip. I would call and plead with him to let me stay in my dorm for the night. He would accuse me of having a date, which was ridiculous, because I rarely talked to girls and never talked to boys. "Hey, whore. Who are you seeing? Come on, you know you're going out with some guy tonight, you fucking skank." I would fight with him till we were both screaming, and then I would give up and make the drive, partly just to spare my roommate. When I would arrive, he would tell me that I made the trip just to cover the fact that I really did have a date. There was no winning. We would fight, we'd have sex, we'd go to bed and the next morning, we would have sex, and I would get back in my car and make my journey back to the school, which was turning into nothing more than a front organization for my relationship with Trent.

My dad faithfully sent me checks of $150 a month. My parents had hoped that I would have a full social life, going out to dinner and seeing movies and attending dances—the usual college stuff. I used every penny of that monthly allowance on gas as I drove to Trent's apartment that was just minutes from my parent's house. Nearly every night, when they thought I was at school having the college experience, I was right under their noses.

My mom would call during the evening, and I wouldn't be there to answer the phone—almost ever. When I would finally call her back, she would wonder how I could be out so much. I would tell her I was either out with my new girlfriends, or at the library studying till late, or doing a project with a classmate. Or, I'd tell her I was at a football game or party. I made it sound like I was living it up. She was usually thrilled. "Just stay up on your grades, Honey," she'd say.

"Of course!"

And somehow, I did, doing most of my studying between classes, in class, at lunch and any moment I could spare. I worked frantically to make sure I had time for Trent. I was near the top of every class, even though I took two hours of nearly every day to drive to Trent's and a couple of hours—each night—to fight. When I would arrive at his apartment, his badgering would start immediately.

You're late.

There was traffic.

At 7:30 at night? Try again.

You know the area. There's always traffic.

Not that much, you fucking liar. Where did you stop?

Nowhere. And I drove as fast as I could. Don't start, alright?

Did you wear that to school today?

No, I changed before I came to see you. Wanted to look nice for you.

Yeah, right. How many guys stopped you and tried to get in your pants today?

What are you talking about? None! I wore jeans and a sweatshirt today.

Listen—I'm not fucking around. Where did you stop?

I didn't stop anywhere—would you please control yourself?

Then why are you so late?

I told you!

You're not going to try to pass off "traffic" again, are you? Do I look stupid?

You know there's such a thing as traffic, right?

Not that much, and don't get mouthy.

Ten minutes isn't that much.

Long enough to stop and make a phone call.

*Would you stop it? That's ridiculous. I'm not lying, Trent. Trust me
    just once, for God's sake.*

Stop treating me like I'm an idiot by lying to me. Then I'll trust you.

*I'm treating you like an idiot? Look, I'm not fighting tonight. Let's
    drop it.*

You haven't been listening to me, have you, you stupid cunt?

I didn't stop anywhere!

Now you're just trying to piss me off.

Can we just drop it and try to have a nice evening?

*It was going to be a nice evening until you came in running your
    lying whore mouth. Just sit and shut up. I'm tired of hearing
    your voice.*

But I...

I told you to shut up!

He would then spend an hour storming around the apartment
talking loudly to himself about the ridiculousness of being with a
lying whore like me.

Are you ready to tell me the truth now? Some nights I would fall
into the trap: I would tell him I had stopped for gas or food just so
he would leave me alone. *I told you that you were a liar! Don't talk to
me for the rest of the night!* And so it would go, every night. Fighting
in between having sex, sleeping, and getting back on the freeway.

Toward the end of the school year, I couldn't take the pace
anymore. I was physically and mentally spent. The entire year felt
like one big fight. I had no friends except for one nice girl down the
hall who invited me to her room now and again. I had experienced
nothing fun—no parties or games or events. One night, lying next
to Trent, I got an idea.

The next day, I looked into colleges closer to my parents' house
that still offered the dorm experience. St. Augustine in San Diego

looked perfect. My plan was to make the case to my parents that it would be the right school for me to transfer to.

"The social scene is better, there are twice as many kids, twice as many things to do, and I think I'll have twice as much fun—you know, a better college experience. My college is nice and all, but there's just not that much to do, too few students, *everyone is really hard to meet because they're so doggone studious.* Plus St. Augustine's sociology department is nationally respected," I told them with great excitement. "Best of all, I can be home with you several times a week!"

They must have thought that perhaps a new crop of less studious kids would increase the chances that a new boy would catch my eye and that, finally, Trent would fall by the wayside.

"Your mother and I talked about it," my dad said, "and we say okay to St. Augustine, but look, stay and live on campus and really sink your teeth into college life. We still want you to have that college experience."

Suckers.

"Oh…well…OK, dad." This was going to be easy. I could still see Trent every night and the drive would only be about 15–20 minutes.

When school started again that fall, Trent and I fell right back into our pattern of going over to his apartment every night and fighting till morning. Sometimes he didn't like my tone on the phone, and we'd fight about that; other times he felt like I wasn't giving him the proper amount of focus, and we'd fight about that. I suppose I could name a couple of other things that might have been sticking points between him and I. However, there was just one argument brewing at the bottom of every spat: He suspected that I was sleeping with some other guy and that I was covering up for him. Trent, utterly convinced of his ability to know the "truth" about what I was doing behind his back, beat that drum so consistently that I truly thought I was losing my mind.

Meanwhile, Trent and his wrestling roommates seemed to be leading a very different life from mine. They were either going to parties or having parties and seemed to have no problem wooing girls to their apartment. There was always a new one or two every time I was over. There were lots of beer cans strewn about and pot paraphernalia everywhere. I noticed that not only did Trent get high almost every night, his beer consumption was reaching crazy levels.

One time I found a used condom under his pillow. "What's this?" I asked.

"Jess, there are dudes bringing girls in and out of here every day," he told me. "That is not mine, and don't ever question me again."

I could feel my blood boil. I started to push the issue, but he blew up fast; I could tell he wanted to squash my surge of curiosity as fast as possible. I had to decide if I wanted to make an issue of it. The truth is, I simply didn't have the energy. How could I look at all the fighting we were doing and sanely decided to add on one more reason to go to battle? I thought about it. *There were tons of people in and out of that apartment; that was true.* I dropped it.

Carly and Diane, the two twin sisters who lived in the room next to me at St. Augustine, were lovely, good-natured girls whom I adored immediately. The three of us hit it off right away and found a few moments here and there to sit and chat. When they would come by to borrow something or ask to have something of theirs delivered to my apartment or have me watch their birds while they were gone, I was always so excited to help. I would open the door to their *yoohoo!* with such delight. They were funny and kind; I couldn't get enough of them. They often wanted to go see a movie or a play at the college theater or run out and get some ice cream. But I always had to tell them no because I was going over to my boyfriend's house. They seemed to always understand until one night, they pressed the issue.

"Jess, what is it with this guy?" they said. "All we're asking you for is a girls' night just once. We'll watch a video and make some popcorn, and it'll be fun. He can't let you go for one night?"

"We're really serious," I told them. "He just really wants to be together, is all." They went back to their room disappointed and I felt sick about it. I really had had just about enough of this crap of having to be at Trent's. I thought, *All I want to do is watch one stinking video and chat with some friends. What is it with him? I've had it up to here. I'm not going to let him push me around anymore. I'm standing up to him!*

"I have a really bad headache," I told him over the phone. "I'm just going to stay in tonight."

"Like hell you do," he said. "You don't have a headache. You're going to get your ass over here."

"Trent, I'm tired and I just want to get some sleep. Come on, it's just one night!"

"Sleep, my ass. You're going to be fucking some other guy tonight and you know it. Don't try to play me for some fool!"

"Look, you'll be alright without me for one night. I just need some sleep so I can kick this thing."

"What's his name? Where did you meet him? Are you just so intoxicating that he has to fuck you tonight?"

"I'm not listening to this anymore," I said. "I told you I'm going to bed early, and that's that. I'll be over first thing in the morning!"

"I don't want some guy's sloppy seconds."

"This is just your imagination, Trent" I said, "You're driving me crazy!"

"Hey Jess, do you have any idea what it is like to be me having to listen to a pathetic person like you lie every two seconds. Every word that comes out of your mouth is another lie. You're disgusting! Now knock this shit off and get your ass over here in 15 minutes or we're going to have problems—do you understand me, you dumb ass?"

"Goodbye, Trent." I said. He was in an expletive-laden rant when I hung up the phone. I was proud of myself and feared for my life all at the same time. But I finally did it. I had defied him.

I went next door. The twins had invited another girlfriend, Sandra, and she had brought her boyfriend, Tommy, and he had brought a buddy of his, Richie, who I had a class with, so I knew of him a bit.

The seven of us were watching TV and eating junk food, and I was giddy with excitement—I could barely contain myself. I felt like I wanted to get everybody into a giant group hug. I was so grateful to hear their voices and hear them laugh and make sarcastic comments at the TV. Everything was the funniest thing I had ever heard. They must have thought, *What's with her?* Just before starting the movie, I got up to go to the bathroom. From there, I heard Carly and Diane's intercom buzz.

It was the angriest buzz I had ever heard.

∞∞∞∞

That's an extraordinary amount of time on the road each day.
Yeah. Nearly two hours. Four hours, really.
You must have done a lot of thinking.
I'm sure I did.
Any memories?
Of what I was thinking about?
Yeah.
What we would do when I got to Trent's, I guess. What we would eat. What we'd fight about, or if I could find a way to avoid a fight. I know I thought a lot about getting there fast. Being late was a disaster.
So that's what you thought about?
Stuff like that.
Nah.
What do you mean?
Well, I'm sure you did think about those things. But there's thinking and there's thoughts, you know?
What's the difference?
Well, thinking is a voice in your head. Your thoughts, well, that's the current going through your heart. Think of it like text and subtext. There's what's said, and then there's what's underneath what's being said.

So you're asking what's the subtext?

    Can you answer that?

I don't know.

    Well, if there was anybody who was pulsing with subtext,
    it was you.

Really?

    Take your time.

Well…I was doing everything I didn't want to do, you know. All that driving. It sucked. I really just wanted to stay in my room. Not have to deal with it. Then all the fighting. Then all that angry sex. I would have liked it if we had a nice night and then had sex. But it was usually like he was punishing me in some way. That sucked. You could almost say I hated him. Does that make any sense?

    Does it to you?

I think it does in some way. He made me feel so…empty. Like I knew there was a strong person inside me, but each time I saw him, he made me question it. I'd say, *Am I really here again?* I was so afraid that the truth was that there really wasn't someone strong in there, and I was just a shell of person. I felt like my only worth was my vagina. He protected it from other boys. We fought over it. He used it. It's really horrible, you know.

    And yet you kept driving.

I did.

    Why? Here you are, a girl full of life. You'd drive 90 miles
    to get it sucked out of you.

Yeah. Guess so.

    You're a normal girl doing an abnormal thing.

It sure stirred up a lot, you know?

    A lot of what?

Well, just a lot. Passion. Anger. Love. Jealousy. Rage. Suspicion. Everything was extended. All the feelings, all the emotions, all the words, all the fighting, all the ranting and raving. Every feeling was extreme. All the veins were popping out, you know. It was like an emotion factory inside Trent's apartment. Or just in his presence. It was really something.

And it all revolved around you.

Yes, it did.

And that felt good.

Yes…it did.

5

THE REAL DEAL,
LITTLE BOY

IN THE FEW HOURS leading up to going over to Carly and Diane's, I was a regular college girl about to do a regular college-girl thing, never mind that I actually had sweaty palms and nervous energy over simply sitting down with some friends to watch a video and eat some junk food. In some ways, however, it felt like my first day of college. All of a sudden, at the sound of a buzzing intercom, it was over. I wasn't a college girl anymore. I was a fugitive.

"Jessica Yaffa there?" the static-heavy male voice said loudly through the intercom.

"Yes," Carly answered back. "Who is this?"

There was no answer.

"Who is this?" she said again into the intercom.

"Oh no," came from my lips while I was in the bathroom. I waited to see if I could hear anything else. When I came out, I asked Carly, "Did you buzz that guy in?"

"No," she said. "Who was that?"

"I'll tell you later."

We all sat down and Diane hit "play" on the machine. Everybody grabbed their snacks and settled in. But I didn't. I knelt down, silent and still. I could feel my heart pumping in my ears. Should I run? Should I hide? My eyes darted around the room. There came a sharp pounding on the door. My heart nearly shot through my chest.

When Carly opened the door, Trent pushed it in from the other side—he had buzzed nearly 120 dorm rooms before finding us—and almost knocked her over. He charged in, eyes smoldering. He looked at me and I flinched.

"Which one of you is fucking my girlfriend?" he yelled.

Everybody erupted, "What's going on here?" "Who are you?"

"Hey, dude. Take it easy," Richie said. "We're just watching a movie. Who are you?"

"So you're the one who wants to get into Jessica's pants, right?" Trent said, taking the chest-filled posture of someone who did not expect to be defied.

"Do you know him, Jessica?" Diane asked.

"Mm hm," I said without taking my eyes off Trent. Just then, Tommy, the starting offensive tackle from the football team, stood up from the couch, all 6'6" and 270 pounds of him. Trent rushed him, and everybody screamed and began to scramble. Tommy grabbed and spun him onto the couch nearly crushing Sandra, who jumped up with a shriek and darted away. Tommy took Trent by the arm and then across the neck and pulled him up straight against his own body. Trent began tussling but wasn't getting anywhere in Tommy's massive arms. Tommy walked him toward the back sliding door and balcony, running into a table and knocking the bowl of chips and all the sodas to the ground as all the girls continued to scream. "Slow down, partner,"

Tommy said. He took Trent outside and shoved him against the corner. "Look, dude," he said with his finger in his face. "I don't know what you think is going on, but we're just a bunch of friends here doing nothing more than watching a movie. Now if you think someone's after your girlfriend, you're wrong about that. So why don't you cool down and get out of here. If you come back, I'm going to hurt you."

After Tommy took his forearm off his chest, Trent stormed back into the room and past everyone who was standing at the sliding glass door watching. "Jessica!" he screamed. He went to the door, opened it and turned to me, "Jessica, let's go." I didn't move. He came and stood over me with all the conviction of a cobra about to strike.

By the look in his eyes, I knew I was totally screwed either way. It didn't matter if I went with him and repented or broke a bottle over his head and ran. He was going to exact a payment from me. It was the maddest I had ever seen him. But I had earned this party. I had done everything he ever wanted me to do, and now I deserved to be here with these people, laughing, eating and wearing my brand-new college sweatshirt. I threw caution to the wind. "Wul, I don't want to go," I said.

"We're leaving!" he yelled and grabbed my arm in a way that felt like he was trying to crush it. I didn't want to continue to ruin Carly and Diane's party, so I stood as he pulled. Some of the girls screamed *no*. Richie grabbed for my other arm. "Jessica?" he said.

"Get your hand off her, asshole!" Trent snapped.

"It's okay, I'm alright." I told Richie.

When we got into the dorm hallway, he slammed the door, walked me down a few apartments and turned and put his hand around the back of my neck, forcing my shoulders to rise. Then he shoved the side of my head against the wall causing a *boom* throughout the entire hallway. "You lying, fucking whore!" he said. "I knew you were lying. I knew I couldn't trust you."

Something moved just down the hall and I looked to see what it was. A little boy appeared from around the vending machine. It was the little brother of our R.A. His eyes went wide with horror as he looked at us. Suddenly, he turned and ran away. I remember thinking, *Yup, this is the real deal, little boy. Run, run as fast as you can.*

Trent turned me around and pushed my face against the rough walls. He squeezed my neck again and forced me down the hall in a hurry, talking the whole time while I winced in pain. "You lying, disgusting fuck of a lying whore," he said. "Damn you, you fucking slut, I ought to kill you." Over and over, without stopping to take a breath, a rat-tat-tat of cursing and threats. He walked me down the stairs and out to his car, slammed me up against it. "Where you taking me, Trent?" I asked him.

"You'll see. Get ready for this, bitch. Get ready for this."

6

THE TRASH-COVERED COUCH

TRENT DROVE WITH THE steering wheel in his left hand and my head in his right. He was gripping and pushing my face into the passenger window of his little, rattle-trap car. "Keep your mouth shut, dumb fuck!" he screamed.

"Trent, no! Please!" I whimpered through a twisted mouth. "He was just trying to protect me. He didn't know who you were! You could have been anybody, right?"

"Bitch! I told you to shut up!" he said as he released my head from the window for a moment only to slam it back again. Beer cans rolled back and forth as his smelly car took corners, his tires squealing around every one. "Whore! Lying whore! This is what happens when whores can't tell the truth! Now this dude thinks he can show himself to me and get away with it? Wait till you see your little lover's fucking party when I get through with him, the fuck."

I was begging and crying as he was about to break my cheekbone on the window, or the window was going to shatter. We screeched to a halt in the oil-stained driveway of his brother's beige-and-light-blue, ramshackle apartment.

"Let's go. Get out of the car." He grabbed me by the hair and pulled me out through the driver's side. "Ouch, ouch, ouch," I cried out. "Trent, please stop!"

"Shut the fuck up!" he said, pulling my face near his. He gave me a sharp shake that yanked my head from side to side.

Bobby was waiting at the top of the landing as Trent pulled me up the stairs. "You got the gun?" Trent said without caring if the neighbors heard. *Gun?* I thought to myself. *Did I just hear him say "gun"?*

"What did this bitch do?" Bobby asked.

"It's for this dude at her school—some big dude who thinks he can show himself to me and get away with it!"

Trent blew past Bobby, kicking the door open with my hair in his hand and pulling me in with him so that I stumbled in sideways. "Better get used to this. You're going to be here a while."

"No gun, T," Bobby said as he came in after us. "You're going to go to jail just because some fucker showed you up? Ain't worth it, man."

"You let me worry about that. Give me the fucking gun."

"Not going to happen, T. You shoot somebody and that gun comes back to me. Forget about it, man," Bobby said. "Just deal with your bitch."

It was at that moment that I got a sense of the length of my punishment. I must have allowed myself to believe that because of the agonizing drive, Trent's constant verbal beat-down and the excruciating hair pulling, enough payment had already occurred and the end might come soon. But now, I understood that it wasn't just punishment that I was going to get, but a sentence. This was going to last.

Trent threw me by my hair onto Bobby's trash-covered couch. He walked in a circle in front of me, slamming his fist against his palm over and over, "Fucking bitch. Fucking bitch. I knew I couldn't trust you. I knew you were a liar. That's all you fucking do is lie. Bitch trying to hook up!"

I sat horrified, looking down as he ranted. At moments I risked a glance at his face. Trent, the person, seemed to be gone. There was only fury.

"Trent," I said.

"Fucking shut up!" he snapped. "You think that now's the time to open your ugly face and talk? Keep your mouth shut, I told you!" He was a foaming, sweaty, sloshing cocktail of embarrassment, vengeance and cheap beer.

He furiously slammed a chair down next to the couch, sat and took a fistful of my hair, pulling it tight from the scalp, lifting the skin from my forehead up toward him. He stuck his face an inch from mine to make each word bite. I could feel his spray on my face. "Skank! Why would these guys defend you if you weren't fucking them? Huh? You say your friend is friends with that guy. That's bullshit. Who are these girls next door? I thought you didn't hang out there. How did you get so chummy, huh? Fucking lying whore. All of a sudden you got all these friends—how is that? This asshole was really sticking up for you. Guys just don't do that. Had sex with him, right? Come out and say it, bitch. 'I had sex with him.' C'mon, it's not that hard. If you didn't fuck him, what did you do? You must have done something, bitch! See, you're just so stupid, Jessica. You're just so stupid!"

The proximity of his face, the feel of his spit, the heat of his breath, the smell of beer in his gut, the pain of my hair separating from my scalp, the ring of my eardrum. It all added up to a kind of searing, almost dissociative pain, as if it were no longer me subject to these horrors, but someone else, some other unlucky girl, a girl I would have told to fight and run if it weren't for the fact that it was *me* being locked in place by a man with a grip of my own thick, brown, curly hair. I tried to keep calm by telling myself it would stop any moment.

"Who else you want to fuck? Huh? Want to fuck Bobby?"

"No," I whimpered.

"He's right here. Say the word, bitch."

"No."

"Really? Cause I happen to know bitches want to fuck, right? Isn't that what whore bitches want to do? Look, I'm just saying what you're thinking. That must be the case, because every time I turn around, you're lying and fucking."

An hour went by, and he was still barking in my ear, a beer in one hand, my hair in the other. Two hours later he was still talking and I had broken into a nonstop cry. Three hours later, he was still talking. He would stand for a moment, circle me, pound his fists and announce to the world what I was, make his way to get a beer and then come back for more. Around two in the morning, Trent went to the bathroom while I collapsed on the couch and shut my eyes. He returned and lifted me off the couch by my hair. "Liars don't deserve to sleep! Wake up!" I felt wetness on my scalp. I was bleeding. He yanked me airborne a dozen times throughout the night.

When the night started, I thought there was no way he could keep this up for an hour. He did it for seven. I saw the sun coming up when I noticed he had fallen to the floor and wasn't getting up. I closed my eyes and finally began to doze off.

A half an hour later, I felt something touch my leg.

7

EAST AND WEST

At first I couldn't tell what was real and what might have been a hallucination. It seemed to go on forever. It started around my calf, a pulling and prodding. Then the feeling moved up my leg to my thigh. Next I felt the drawstring to my sweatpants being loosened. Suddenly I was clearer about what was going on. Trent was rummaging through the spoils. I lay still on the couch, kept my eyes closed and began to pray. *Please, God, no. Please don't let him do this.* He began to pull my clothes off slowly—as if he expected that I might actually stay asleep. He wasn't aggressive, but methodical. My heart shuddered, horrified in my chest. I had to think quickly. If I fought, would he hurt me? But if I gave in, would he think I was okay with what he had just done and what he was about to do?

I came up with an idea. I would protest by simply lying there and give him nothing. No life, no words, no opened eyes. It would be just him, his conscience, and my body. But I wouldn't be there.

When he was spent, he fell back with his full weight into a trashy sofa chair that skidded on the carpet. He panted and shook with aftershocks of his deed. I laid there feeling like road kill. I reached up and scratched just above my left ear; it hurt like I had been kicked in the head. I wriggled my sweatpants around my waist and looked back at him, sat up, and started to cry. He didn't say anything.

"I'm done," I said, having no idea where my thoughts might take me. "I'm done feeling like this. I'm done not being enough, and I'm done having to prove myself to you. I have no life and I have no friends. It was one night, and it was a movie and it turned into this, and there was a gun, for God's sake. I'm sorry, I can't do this."

I stopped and looked down, a little surprised that a list of my thoughts fell from my mouth without me having to make any effort to summon them—they were just there. I looked up. I looked at him. I was about to witness the full swing of his depravity, the east and west of Trent.

He covered his face with his hand and his knee began to shake up and down. Then from somewhere deep inside, like a teapot of boiling water, he began to wail uncontrollably. It was a disturbing, sorrowful cry. Tears aggressively rolled down his cheeks. He fell to the ground and came to me on his hands and knees.

"I was drunk and out of control. I have a drinking problem. Give me another chance, please. I'm done drinking. I'm so sorry. Please don't leave me. I've never treated you like this before. I've never touched you, and I've been mad plenty of times. It has to be the alcohol. My dad's a raging alcoholic. You don't know what he's like, but he is. He starts drinking and he gets out of control. He'll beat the shit out of you. You have no idea."

I looked in his face. Trent had gone from my torturer to a scared child in a matter of seconds.

"And I've heard it's hereditary, so I must be an alcoholic, too. If I have to go to AA, I will. And if I have to see a counselor, I will, tomorrow! Please, please don't leave me. I've never done it before.

It's not a pattern or anything. I love you. I promise I will never do this again."

I was resolved before he spoke. Suddenly, I felt my resolve slipping away. In just a few moments, I felt desperately alone. I was certain I was right about being finished with Trent after what he had just done, but I felt hopeless without him. It seemed the hole in my heart, the one that I had carried with me since I was a little girl, suddenly stretched and wrenched and called attention to itself, saying, *Remember me. You have to deal with me.*

And just like that, mere seconds after I made my resolute declaration, something within me reached to fill the hole. I started to think, *Hmm. He's right. He never has done that before. He's been mad plenty of times, but he's never done that. It must have been the alcohol. He has been drinking a lot lately. Maybe if he doesn't drink, it will be okay. Maybe it was because this time he was drinking all through the night and he really had no control. And if his dad is an alcoholic, then how can he really help it but to be one, too? I have never seen him so sorry. He's saying he won't drink anymore.*

"I can't make a decision today," I said, "I'm not ready. But I want you to get some help."

"Take all the time you need!" he said, his face filled with tears and the hope that I might remain his girl. "I'm going to get some help. I understand you're upset and shaken. You have the right to be scared. I'm just going to work on myself and you can take all the time you need. You're right about everything. I did something wrong and that is not okay. You don't deserve this."

My Roman holiday, when I was curled up, sobbing on the floor of the hotel room, flashed through my mind. My dad and Sam playing catch in the front yard just moments after my dad said he didn't have time for me, did too. All the times when I was begging, and my dad just didn't seem to love me enough to give me any attention came cascading over me. That's what I knew of men. Except for now. I was hearing something different. Because, as the days went by, Trent did everything I said I wanted with immediacy and urgency. Counselors. AA meetings. Flowers. Humor. Kind speech. Consideration. He was putting me first.

The weeks that followed were some of the best of my life. I had meals with my girlfriends. He didn't grill me over what I did or whom I was with. He made me dinners. He gave me flowers in a vase. He told me he loved me. I told him I loved him, too. He hugged me tenderly and made no demands on my time. I could not have been happier. Everything felt right. I looked in his eyes and felt certain he had really changed.

I was leaving his apartment early one morning. We were holding hands on our way out to my car when I stopped to dig in my purse for my keys. "I'm having dinner with Carly and Diana tonight."

"You are?"

"Yeah. I told you a while back. Remember?" He looked at the ground. Then he looked off to the side at nothing in particular. He took a moment.

"You had dinner with them last week," he said.

"Yeah, I know."

"Well how often do you have to see these friends?" Like a crack of thunder before a deluge begins, I knew I had heard something that spelled trouble.

That night at dinner with Carly and Diana, I found myself not as carefree as I had become in recent weeks. My mind drifted. Laughs were a bit harder to come by. I knew all of the time spent with the girls and the other things that I had come to enjoy were coming to an end.

And sure enough, a day later, the rain clouds opened up.

You've had lunch with them every day this week—why can't you be here by five? It's 5:07. Did you stop somewhere along the way? You don't have any gas. You had half a tank yesterday. If you really just came back and forth from my house, you should have much more than that. Where else did you go? Did you stop somewhere else? Have you found somebody else?

I tried to push back, to rescue all the progress that we had made. At first, he seemed to expect some give and take; he would tolerate me speaking my mind and making the argument that our lives were better with a little space between us, and a fuller social life for me made me a happier person for him to be with. But soon, none of that mattered. He began to try to squelch any resistance.

"Look," he said. "I want you here by five o'clock—no questions asked!"

I refused the thought of being pushed around. I was going to fight for the gains we had made. And fight we did. Suddenly, we were back on familiar ground. There were nightly screaming matches that lasted three to four hours—often into the next morning. There were threats and vile name-calling and mind-bendingly illogical arguments. They were nasty and hateful and depleting. When I was with him, I could smell a mix of beer and pot on his breath. Each fight, no matter the starting point, always led to Trent suspecting I either was with someone else or wanted to be.

My body and mind felt emptied; by that point, I had used up even my reserve energy to keep up with Trent's anger. My brain was trying to shut off the noise of Trent's constant voice; I began to make decisions out of self-protection. I started to follow his instructions down to the smallest detail. I would get to his apartment right after school, just like before. I also returned to calling him multiple times a day so he would know where I was at all times. After all, it was my behavior that always seemed to be causing the problems.

Weeks went by, and suddenly I looked up, and our relationship had reverted to exactly where it was before Trent crashed our girls' night out. I had lost. I saw it coming and I still couldn't do anything about it. I looked out the window one morning and found myself in a strange, hour-long fantasy about life without Trent. It seemed so delicious. My heart and soul were pleading for an end to all this. For a short time while Trent seemed to be rehabilitating, I bathed in rays of hope. Now all of that light was extinguished. Was now the time it would come to an end? Was this the window of time that I should step through and claim my life back? Was I really going to break up with Trent?

A day later, when I was home for a visit, my mom asked me to come into her bedroom after I finished taking a shower. Suddenly, it was clear—the window had closed.

∞∞∞∞

I should have walked away when I had the chance, right?

Depends.

On what?

Well, it depends on whether or not you really had a chance.

To leave?

Yeah.

Well, of course I had a chance. I mean, I was ready to walk away, and he knew I was ready to walk away. That's why he started crying. I should have just left.

It may not be that you really had what you thought you had. Maybe it didn't matter what you did.

What do you mean?

Well maybe he could have cried, or he could have demanded that you stayed, or threatened you if you left, or talked you into staying—you know, different things. And you might have still returned. In other words, it might not have mattered what you said or did, or even that he cried, if you're suggesting you stayed because you felt sorry for him.

You mean I was destined to go back to him?

Well, I don't know. I just wonder if maybe the injury you sustained early in your life was the determining factor and not what Trent did. I mean being abandoned by your dad is deep. These circumstances are not. You didn't go back to him because you felt sorry for him. You weren't even operating at that level.

What level was I operating at?

Shattered.

8

MELANOMAS AND ANACONDAS

"HI, HONEY, COME ON IN," my mom said. She was sitting in a love seat by her bedroom window with a blanket on her lap. It looked as though she had been there a while.

"What's up?" I asked.

"Have a seat, sweetie," she said. She looked at me a bit. As I walked in, she looked outside the window. She cleared her throat.

"You said you wanted to talk to me?" I offered.

"Well, yes, I do." Her voice sounded odd. Her face looked tired. "I have a bit of news for you." Nothing about her face made me feel like I wanted to hear it.

"Doesn't sound like good news," I said.

She sat there for a moment.

"It's not."

Dad's stubborn little "racquetball injury" that didn't want to heal was diagnosed as melanoma. It was aggressive and time was short.

He was admitted into the hospital, and just like that, right in the middle of a rather normal life, everything started to roll away from us—as if we were invisible to God. The disease mattered and we didn't. All the test results were bad. All the diagnoses were bleak. Dad was going to die.

I regularly went to his side as he rested on the couch. I would look at the fear in his eyes and watch my chance for meaning slip away.

Immediately after dad was admitted to the hospital, my mom, brother, and I assumed a new role in his life: visitor. I suppose in some ways I was trying to be strong for him. Encouraging. Positive. But underneath it all, I had a different goal. Every minute with him was spent trying to clear away the brush of the past—so I could see that I did indeed make it into his heart. I was desperately angling for the smallest sentiment that daddy's little girl delighted him in some way. I would have taken anything.

Dad closed his eyes more frequently as his body was starting to shut down, little by little, inch by agonizing inch. I was essentially perishing alongside my dad. If he went, I went. He held the keys to me.

Trent was understanding and supportive. He rubbed my back when I looked at my dad and held me close as I cried. He got up to get me something to drink. His touch was soft and caring. He kissed away my tears.

My mother was barely keeping it together. Sam was a lifeless mess. My dad was wasting away—occupying less and less space in his hospital bed. I felt myself slip beneath the fear, as if being submerged in it. I needed something or someone to take over for me, to begin where I ended, and Trent was there. For all his anger and vise-like control, there was nothing about him that I needed to guess about. He was my certainty when everything else was uncertain. I clung to his muscular body. When he took hold of me, it was all business. He was my protector. I began to see him as a great rock rising out of the sea—rugged, unrefined and immovable. He was my survival.

I never expressed that to him, however. Something in him just instinctively knew that it was time to press in—to become more of who he was, to reveal more of the madness that was inside of him and take more of what he wanted from me. Like an anaconda snake with his body around its prey, he could feel me exhale. Then he squeezed.

It began to happen when he grew frustrated with the amount of time I was spending at my dad's bedside. There was no way to contact me in dad's room, and without access, Trent's mind began to spin out. He believed that I was out having sex any time I was not with him. I do not think he was just saying it to keep control—it wasn't merely a tool. Trent had the capacity for unfathomable levels of suspicion. He believed that I was in bed with doctors or other visitors to the hospital. So he began to tighten his hold. He started by trying to break me down.

How do I know you're really at the hospital? How do I know you're not in bed with somebody over there? There are guys around—I know there are. You say you're at the hospital, but you could be in your dorm room fucking somebody else. You were just at the fucking hospital last night. You need to go again? Your dad's unconscious; he doesn't know you're there. Do you really need to be there if he can't talk to you? Isn't your mom there? You all have to be there? This is bullshit. You're not going to the hospital. Where are you really going? You were there three hours? What are you doing for three hours at the hospital with an unconscious man who can't even talk to you? I don't believe you, you whore. Get your lying ass over here and don't make me wait.

Next, he instituted a new edition of non-negotiable rules. I had to call before I left the hospital, and then call again the moment I got to my parents' house. Total allowable time: 17 minutes. Then he'd keep me on the phone as he picked fights with me into the morning hours so that he would know I didn't have time to be in bed with someone else.

If I was going straight to his apartment from the hospital, I had to call before I left and walk inside his door no later than 11 minutes after the call. When I would walk in the door of his apartment, he would look at his watch and then silently walk right past me with pen and paper in hand and run down to check the mileage of my car. He was monitoring me down to the mile. There was no talking to him prior to getting the reading off the odometer. Until he checked, I was in trouble. I hated it.

However, he was just getting warmed up. If I was a minute late, or if there were too many miles on my odometer, there would be "fucking hell to pay." On the night a fire hydrant flooded the streets, it slowed my frantic drive and I was late getting to his apartment. Total time: 15 minutes—four minutes over. He grabbed me by the neck with his left hand, shoved my head against the nearest wall so forcefully that it produced a resounding boom throughout the apartment. He then hit the wall with his right fist, right alongside my head.

Of course, the fact that his outbursts didn't deter my devotion only meant that I was ready for the anaconda to give another squeeze.

He graduated to taking my jaw in his hand and pinching so hard my lips would contort and split as he spit in my face. "Fuck you!" His voice was so loud, I felt like he was inside my head. "Don't ever forget to call me again. When you don't call, it means you're fucking around. You think I don't know that?"

Spit.

It was a Monday at around four in the afternoon. I had stopped by his apartment before going to the hospital. Trent had decided he was going to come with me, so he took a quick shower. The doorbell rang, and I answered it. A guy tried to sell me magazines. I gave him my excuse as to why we would not be buying. The guy tried to work around my reasoning, but in the end, I wasn't going to relent, and I said goodbye and that I wished him luck in making sales. I shut the door. Trent came from the room red in the face. I had "disrespected him" by "talking flirtatiously" to the guy. I thought it was just another accusation. It wasn't. He stepped into a backhand so hard that as his knuckles made contact with my face, my nose exploded all over the wall. I lay on the floor and watched the red blood drip down the beige paint.

He stood over me. "You dumb ass! You don't know how to treat a man. A real woman doesn't talk to other men. A real woman doesn't fuck other men. A real woman shows respect and knows her place. If any man knew how dirty and pathetic and stupid you were, nobody would give you the time of day. They would just use you for the fucking dumb fuck you are. You're lucky you have me. What would you do without me, you fucking poor excuse for a woman? You ain't shit and you'll never be shit."

Spit.

I lay there with tears, blood and his saliva running down my face. I could feel the pain inside my head and the dripping sensation along my ear. That's when a strange series of thoughts seeped into my mind, like passing billboards along a highway.

How could he?

I felt the blood's stickiness in my hand; I could barely breathe through my nose.

I know not to break his rules. Why in the world do I do it?

I heard myself pant and blood gurgling in my throat. I touched my nose and it felt like it had been repositioned to the left.

He's told me before not to talk to men. How stupid could I be?

My head, just behind my eyes, began to fill with pressure like it was going to explode.

If only I could prove to him that I could be trusted.

Trent went over to the door, stormed out and slammed it as if he were trying to bring down the entire apartment.

I'm sure he hates having to hit me.

He was right about his assumption—absolutely right. It didn't matter if I liked how he treated me or not. I was without an anchor. So if he wanted to squeeze, what was I going to do about it?

In my dad's last weeks, I went to his bedside less and less. Trent demanded that I give up my vigil—besides, he needed sex every night, no questions asked. It didn't matter if I was exhausted, grieving, sick or menstruating. I would tell my mom that the reason I wasn't with her and my dad was because I was busy with school activities and projects. She saw them as good distractions from all that was going on at the hospital, which was my dad's slow winding-down.

I was lying to my mother about where I was, but I was once again lying to my dad, too. Mom would answer the phone in the hospital room and say to dad, "Jessica's busy with school, darling, isn't that great? She wants to say hi." She would put the phone to my dad's ear, and I would say through guilty tears to the man I loved so much, "…Hi daddy, I love you…I hope you're comfortable today…You're going to be better real soon, you'll see…You're so strong, daddy…I know you're going to bounce back…Goodnight…I love you."

I would hang up the phone, walk over and sit next to Trent watching TV. It was right where he wanted me. I kept my head toward the TV but strained my eyes to look sharply to the left at Trent, his eyes fixed on his show, his mouth breaking open in laughter, the crumbs on his chin. He knew I didn't like this show, but I had to sit there right next to him. I couldn't be over there at the table doing my homework or at the window reading a book. I had to be there, wedged between him and the arm of the couch watching a stupid situation comedy while at the hospital, my mom was sitting next to my dad, giving him what healing there was in her presence. In my mind, I could see the chair on the other side of dad, the one with the purple material, and no one in it. It made me feel sick to my stomach. I was giving up on my dad.

My dad died on November 22, 1995. The staff at the hospital had prepared us and we had done what we could to prepare ourselves. We knew he was going to die for quite some time and yet we were still shocked and devastated.

I cried bitterly for the loss of my beautiful dad, for my mom, who lost her best friend, for my brother, who lost his hero and biggest supporter—and for the crazy-haired little girl who never did get to fall breathlessly into his arms.

The night before the funeral, Trent called to say he didn't have a ride to the service. I didn't think twice. I immediately went into my normal fix-it mode. If he needed me, I was always going to help. I told him that the next morning I'd call my friends who were coming to the funeral and ask them to give him a ride. It was an absurd thing to offer, considering what the day held for me. It was even more absurd that he would say, "Okay, go ahead." Sitting in my dress with tissue in hand, it took me nearly an hour to track somebody down.

The morning of the funeral was beautiful. The sun was out, the sky was a piercing blue and the shadows were cold. Dad's law firm attended en masse plus friends and associates as well as our family from Boston. It was a lovely service on a lovely day, and I cried from the moment I got up until the time they laid dad in the ground. Trent was right by my side at every moment. He seemed a bit on edge. I just chalked it up to being around lots of people he didn't know.

Everyone was invited to my mother's house for a reception after the service and Trent was not planning to go. I had already spent much of the morning arranging for his ride home, but he noticed that there seemed to be lots of young men who might be coming to the house, and he didn't like that. Suddenly he said he was coming. He told me that I might have had a past with one or more. "I haven't," I told him.

"Shut up."

My mother had arranged for my family to be seated at the couch near the doorway to allow us to greet each person who came to the reception and give them a chance to offer their condolences. We ended up standing as each person wanted to give us a hug.

Trent was uncomfortable with the hugging and sat on the couch beside me as I stood. His body was tense, and his eyes were alert as he leaned in closely, ready to break up a hug that he thought lasted too long. I noticed his body get rigid as he watched, hands slightly raised, ready to jump in. He didn't want to meet anybody, so I stopped introducing him. By the way he was making everybody feel with his coiled posture, I'm pretty sure nobody wanted to meet him, either.

My mom, who would rather Trent not be there at all, gave me an incensed look every time she turned her head my way. It was as if to say, "What the hell is going on over there?"

Afterward, mom said nothing about it, but I knew what her looks were trying to convey, "Good Lord, young lady. How could you let something like that happen?" Of course, that was the one-thousandth time I had seen it.

The days and weeks passed, and I knew it was time that I have a sit-down with my mom and tell her the next piece of news that was going to shatter her world. It was about a month and a half after the funeral that I asked my mom to meet me for dinner, and I dreaded the thought of it. I arrived at the restaurant and took a deep breath as I scanned the crowd, touching my bulging stomach, now two months into its transformation. I figured if I told her in a public place, it would cut down on the hysteria.

She was already seated when I spotted her. She was still in deep mourning over my dad. I could read it on her face. She had lost

15 pounds off her already-tiny frame. I was so nervous, eating was the last thing I wanted to do. I ordered a house salad so I didn't have to look at the menu. Mom finished ordering and put the napkin on her lap as the waiter walked away.

"How are you, honey?" she asked.

"I'm good, you know, all things considered," I answered. I could feel my expression betray that what I had just said was a lie. The truth was, I was scared to death. "Hey, mom," I said. "Listen, there's something I need to tell you." I paused for a second to gather my courage. I was looking down, and when I peered through the tops of my eyes, she was already shaking her head in disbelief. I just watched her for a second or two as she tried in those few moments to make it all go away. I gave her a guilty smile and began to nod my head as if to say, *Oh yes I am.*

"Oh, Jess. Please no," she said with pleading in her voice. "Tell me you're not."

"I'm sorry, mom." I offered. "But it's going to be okay."

"Honey," she said, turning white before my eyes. She didn't finish her sentence.

"Mom, look—."

"Jessica. I'm not in any position to raise a child. And you're not either!"

"I'm not asking for your help."

"But how do you think you're going to do it? Alone? Honey, you'll be all alone."

"Look, mom, I want the baby, and Trent wants the baby; it's a big shock now, but it will be okay, you'll see. Trent and I will raise the baby—it'll be fine."

"Think about it for a minute. How can this be good for the baby? Look at your life. Neither of you have any money. Trent has no career, no education, no direction. He still hasn't even figured out how to treat you. What kind of life are you two going to offer that child? What about you? You think raising a child is all hugs and kisses and cute clothes? It's not! You'll need help. You think Trent is going to be there to help you? Honey, I'm scared to death for the baby and for you!"

I fully believed she cared about the well-being of the baby, but she was skimming the surface of what was really on her mind. I shot her a *you-make-me-so-mad* look.

"And a baby is going to tie you to Trent for the rest of your life!" she said.

"That's what this is really about, isn't it?"

"It's about all of it!"

I leaned aggressively. "Well, it's already done!"

We were getting loud and we had just started. We sat in silence for a moment, trying to appear to everyone else in the room that we were under control. I looked away from her. "I don't know what we're fighting for, mom. I'm having the baby and that's that," I said in a quiet smolder.

I ate exactly two bites of my salad, and mom ate none. The evening was a disaster. My mom, disappointed and scared as she was, was able to fight through her emotional state to hug me before we departed in the parking lot and tell me she loved me.

"I appreciate it, mom," I said. "We'll be alright."

"Jessica," she said as she looked me in the eye. "I don't think you understand just how alone you're going to be."

A day later I got a call from Sam, now 13 years old and already crying when I answered. "This is terrible, what you've done," he said with sniffles. "You're an embarrassment."

He hung up, and, with the phone still in my hand, I caught a glimpse of myself in the mirror. I looked so ugly. I don't know that I had ever seen myself quite that ugly before. I was hideous. I was an embarrassment. I was a disappointment. I was a fool. I was dirty.

I put the phone down and got in my car and went over to see Trent, my drug. I opened the door to his apartment. "I thought you were supposed to be here at 2 o'clock," he said.

"I came early."

"Why?"

"I wanted to see you."

"You sure you didn't come over to make yourself feel better?" he asked.

"About what?" I snapped back. I was in no mood.

"You must have been fucking somebody. You fucking somebody?"

"That's ridiculous!" I yelled back at him. "I just wanted to be with you!"

"Like hell!"

"Like hell? What about all of the girls you have over here all the time? What's that all about?"

"I told you they're Juan and Jeff's girls—I got nothing to do with them! And don't ever question me about them again—I already told you that, bitch!" He turned and with a short, blinding fist, he slammed his knuckle against my mouth, splitting my lip and loosening my teeth. I tumbled to the ground.

"What are you doing?" I screamed.

"You think you can talk to me that way? I ain't taking shit from no stupid, dumb, fucking whore. Have to teach you how to talk to a man!" he said as he grabbed me by the hair and pulled me toward him.

"Please don't, Trent!" I shrieked as I tried to wrestle my hair out of his grip. In an instant he put his hand on the back of my neck and squeezed so hard I thought my eyes were going to tumble from my head. He threw me toward his couch face first, and my knees hit the ground and skidded. He pulled my pants down, and I screamed.

"Shut up, slut!" he said as he slapped the side of my head, making my ears ring.

He wasn't going to have sex with me, he was going to punish me—a very bad girl with a disrespectful mouth. With his hand forcing my face into the couch cushions to muzzle me, he ripped me apart. Like a wounded animal fighting to stay alive, he grunted and groaned and whimpered as he sodomized me. I screamed and almost bit a hole in the fabric of his couch. I actually thought what he was doing was going to kill me. It went on so long I stopped screaming and just sobbed. He was going to finish his business and nothing I did was going to stop him.

When it was over, he stumbled away with a disgusting, drowsy look on his sweaty face and pulling up his pathetic pants.

I lay there with my mind swirling in a haze of pain, shame and disbelief. He went to the bathroom. When he came out, he didn't talk to me. He lay on his couch as if nothing happened and watched TV. I heard him begin to snore.

Later that day, I sat by his kitchen window, rubbing my belly and looking out at the street below. Dusk caused the street lamps to flicker as they turned on. Trent was storming around the apartment mad at something. Me. The World. It didn't matter. I was living a crazy existence. Yet something about it made a strange, perverted sense. My father was gone. My mom was emotionally gone. My brother didn't want anything to do with me. I had no friends. My Catholic college would soon ask me to leave the campus while I was pregnant, as was their policy. As I looked at Trent, pacing around me like a guard dog—growl and all—I thought of my mom saying, "I don't think you understand just how alone you're going to be." But I wasn't going to be alone.

I had Trent.

9

DAYDREAM
IN THE CHAPEL

"Do you, Trent, take Jessica as your lawfully wedded wife?" the Justice of the Peace asked. Trent and I faced each other at the front of an empty, cheap Las Vegas chapel in the middle of a scorching day, with sunrays beaming through the windows onto the red carpet.

"I do," Trent said. I looked into his eyes and couldn't tell if what I saw was love or appetite.

I looked down. I shook my head subtly in disbelief.

I didn't know that it was possible for a heart to hold such competing emotions all at once. At the same time that I had seen Trent's dark and violent side, the other side of him was everything I wanted. He was absolutely, singularly focused on me. All his passions, all his desires, all his goals and dreams drained into one. It felt good in some ways—many ways, in fact. And he had given me a beautiful boy and a bit of hope. That is why I was standing there in the white dress that I had worn to Sam's bar mitzvah. I was rooting for hope to win over my doubts.

Yet, it was daunting to be someone's everything. Could I live up?

My eyes darted around the red carpet, pausing for a moment on my white shoes, my head still slightly moving back and forth. I thought of everything that had happened over the last year, and our son, Rory, who, just months old, was staying with Trent's parents in San Diego.

The weeks and months after my pregnant belly really began to protrude were good between us. Trent would lie in bed with me and rub my belly and talk to the baby, telling him how excited he was to meet him.

"Hey, little guy," he would say, "I know you can't hear me, but I hope you can feel me in your heart. I hope you know how beautiful you are to your mom and dad and how much you're going to be loved. I can't wait to see you and pick you up and show the world my strong boy. I'm counting the days."

It was beautiful to see. He would kiss my stomach and I would stroke the back of his head. I could feel my hope swell. He kissed my skin in a way that he never kissed my lips; so slowly and so lightly. His fingers glided along the curvature of my body like he was calling forth life. His eyes would well up. He filled the room with his soft voice that was so soothing. I believed in Trent. I believed in his love. I believed a baby could help us set a new course. Of course, that was just before he would lay me back and do his nightly business. I had thought the pregnancy might create a pause in Trent's sexual hunger. But he even said it was a turn-on to do it with a pregnant woman. There was no winning.

We were living in a tiny apartment not far from my school where I was still taking classes toward my degree in sociology. Trent had taken a job as a security guard and he trudged off to work dutifully. He had the baby and me to support, he proudly would proudly say.

As I grew larger, the mirror grew more painful for me to pass by. Everything about me was expanding or changing: my hair looked awful, my eyes were puffy, my skin was blotchy, my lips were swollen. Things I had heard about pregnant women becoming glowing beauties did not apply to me. I wanted someone to talk to about it; maybe they could tell me it was all in my mind. But I had no one to call. Sometimes I would sit in the silence of the apartment and just look around, running over and over in my mind the ridiculousness of a girl living in a city of millions of people and having absolutely no one to talk to. The talkative girl who had lots of friends now lived in quiet obscurity.

But isolation and growing girth weren't my only problems. Not only was I completely friendless, it occurred to me that, as a 20-year-old pregnant student who sits inside her apartment and talks to no one but her own belly, there were very few girls in the world who were like me. I wasn't just alone. I was an oddity. My self-worth evaporated.

Somewhere toward the middle of my last trimester, the Trent that seemed rather happy for the past five months began to slip away.

"Look at this fucking place!" he would scream. "It's a fucking pigsty! Pick it up!"

My mom had never required much from me with respect to keeping a neat room or tidy house—it could have been because of my complete rebellion to lift a finger—so when it came to suddenly maintaining my own place, I was woefully underprepared. I had never even changed a vacuum cleaner bag before. Even so, Trent's reactions to my efforts, poor as they might have been, were completely out of balance.

"You call this carpet clean?" he said just a few hours after I had vacuumed it.

"I don't see what's so dirty about it," I replied.

He grabbed me by the hair, forcing me to the ground. "You don't see it, you fucking dummy? Come here, then." He would put his hand around the back of my neck and push my face to the carpet. "See it now, bitch? See it now? That's dirt. Clean it!"

Every day while Trent was away, it became a rush to clean the house so pristinely he would have no complaints. And yet, every day he would walk in the house and, without really even looking around, declare it filthy.

"You fucking, dumb, lazy ass. You can't even do the smallest thing. What kind of mother are you going to be? One who can't even keep a tiny apartment clean? You think my boy is going to grow up in a filthy house? Are you that stupid? Are you that worthless?"

I would look at what he was screaming about. I couldn't figure out what he was seeing. I thought maybe he was right—maybe I was too stupid to know what clean really was. So I committed to doing an even better job. Every single day, whether I had done it the day before or not, I would mop the floors, scrub every counter, dust every piece of electronics, wipe all the appliances, vacuum all the drapes, clean the toilets and shower and wipe down walls.

Still he would walk in the house, and before he would say hello, he would start in on me about how awful of a person I was that I didn't care about anybody but myself.

"What do you think this is? You've got a baby on the way, and you keep a house like this? You are the worst fucking excuse for a mother I've ever seen, you pathetic piece of shit!"

So I decided I would scrub the grout, pull out the electronics and dust underneath and behind, clean windows inside and out, straighten and wipe down the refrigerator, scrub beneath all appliances, polish silverware, bowls and dishes, clean on the tops of doors and polish handles. I was making myself sick with exhaustion.

It didn't work.

"Fuck you! Can't you get anything right? Are you going to go through your entire life and never do anything above shitty? Huh? Answer me!"

"I worked really hard, Trent," I would say, trying to hold back the tears.

"And you can't see how fucked up you are? Well, you better work harder then, dumb fuck!" He would usually give me a last good shake of the arm or squeeze of my face and storm off. I would take a seat somewhere, anywhere, and cry before getting back to trying to find some dirt, *any* dirt to clean. *I must really suck,* I remember thinking to myself. I usually stopped cleaning around 4 o'clock so I could concentrate on making dinner, which I usually did in a state of panic. Before I had moved in with Trent, I hadn't so much as made scrambled eggs.

"Where did you get this, out of a can of dog food?" he would say as he looked at the dinner I set in front of him.

"No. It's from a package I bought at the store."

"Well did you read it, or did you just gloss over it like you do everything else?"

"No, I read it."

"You mean it tells you how to do it step by step, and you still cooked it into a pile of dog shit?"

"But you haven't even tasted it yet."

"I don't have to! Look at it. Can't you do the easiest thing? Are you really that thick in the head?" he said with an intense and shaking index finger to his own temple. "C'mon, tell me you're not that fucking dumb? *Please* tell me you're not that fucking dumb?" he yelled, this time holding his index finger to my head.

Nearly every reaction to every meal was the same. He called it garbage, or worse, and told me I was the kind of mother who would feed her baby food that would kill him.

"I have to have you up to speed, Jessica. My baby is coming soon, and you still can't cook shit."

One Saturday afternoon I was exhausted and thought I might try to take a nap since he had stepped out to the store. When he walked in the door, I was in a deep sleep. He saw me on the couch and lifted me by my hair. "Get your lazy ass in the kitchen and make me dinner!" he slurred.

I didn't have anything prepared for that night, hoping that we might go to McDonald's. I took some leftover chicken that he hadn't touched the night before and did my best to try and give it a new spin with onions and spices from the cupboard.

When he sat down, I placed the chicken dish in front of him and he grabbed a handful of it and smashed it in my face, then batted the rest to the floor. "A real woman doesn't give her man leftovers, bitch! Now clean it up!"

I knelt down on the floor that I had polished to a fine shine earlier that day and began to put the food in a trashcan. I cried and touched my belly. "I'm sorry, honey," I said to my baby, sniffling as I cleaned. "I'm so sorry I'm bringing you into all this. I'm going to do everything I can to give you a happy life."

The baby had become my only friend. I talked to him incessantly. I felt that I wasn't even really living for me anymore, but entirely for him. I couldn't wait to see him and kiss his cheeks and have him need and love me.

"Mommy can't wait to see you, sweetie," I whispered to him while I lay in bed and looked at the moon in our bedroom window. "You and me, we're going to have so much fun. And don't you worry about your mommy. Maybe I'm just getting what I deserve and it's time to become a better person. Sometimes I am a little slow in getting stuff."

The night that I delivered after nine hours of labor and a C-section, Trent cried without restraint. When he gently took our baby from my arms and held him close, tears streamed down his face. "I want to call him Rory. Is that okay?" he asked. They looked utterly adorable, my two boys crying together. "That's fine," I said, glowing.

Rory was a little dark jewel, more beautiful than even I had fantasized. I was overcome with love for him and for Trent too, who, when not kissing Rory, was kissing my hand or my forehead.

"Babe, listen to me," he said softly as he looked into my eyes. "You were so beautiful when you were giving birth. I have new respect for you. And I want you to know this. I am going to be a better dad to Rory than my dad was to me. And I am going to be so different to you, too. I know I have put you through a lot and you never deserved any of it, and I am so sorry. I'm going to be better, you'll see. I love you and we are going to be so happy together. The three of us will be so happy."

He showered me with kisses and lay on the thin edge of the hospital bed to hold me as close as possible.

"Beautiful Jessica," he whispered. "Beautiful, beautiful Jessica."

In my entire life, I hadn't been quite so happy. Everything seemed worth it to be there, cradled by my man as I cradled my baby boy. *Rory deserves a mother and father who are married,* I thought to myself. *I'm going to do right by him.*

"And do you Jessica, take Trent as your lawfully wedded husband?" the Justice of the Peace asked me.

I looked at Trent, my son's father.

"I do."

∞∞∞∞

How long did he wait after the baby?
For what?
I think you know what I'm talking about.
To have sex with me?
Mm hm.
The doctor told us to wait at least six weeks.
So how long did he wait?
Two weeks.
And what happened the first night you got home?
He demanded oral sex.

10

DEMONS IN THE CATHEDRAL

It makes me think of this quote I heard, "Even the smallest glimmer of hope shines like the sun." Something like that.
That applies to me?

It applies to all women who have been through what you have been through.
How so?

Well, you're so starving for love, you'll take all that your abuser dishes out, and as long as he does something nice for you or he impresses you in some way—like crying over the baby—you'll think you can build a life on that, forgoing all the pain he has caused you. It's a super-strong impulse.
I guess I was determined to stack the pieces in a way that best suited me. You just want to believe, you know? I guess you think I'm crazy to marry him after he hit me in the nose and had sodomized me. But

the way I saw it, it had been a long time since he had done anything too violent and after Rory was born, what he said about being happy together and the fact that he hadn't hit me for a while really made me believe that he was trying to turn things around, even though he was freaking out about the apartment.

> Listen, I do not think you're crazy. I'm not here to judge you in that way. I'm just stating a fact. Sometimes women who are abused go into the mode of trying to save their lives. The mind will go through somersaults to try to do it.

Somersaults. That's a good way to describe me. I didn't know which way was up and which way was down, you know? I felt like I was tumbling around. Does he love me? Does he hate me? Does he even care?

> Now, that I don't believe.

You don't? Why not?

> Because deep down, you knew he never loved you.

He didn't?

> The one thing you believed about yourself more than anything was that you were not lovable.

I wasn't?

> Think about it. You said you told your baby that perhaps, *you were getting what you deserve.*

That's true.

> If you ever believed for a second that you were lovable, that statement would have never come out of your mouth, no matter what.

Why wasn't I lovable?

> You were.

Why didn't I believe it?

> Do you really need to ask?

So if your dad never loves you, no one else can, either?

∞∞∞∞

"How many are you going to have?" I asked Trent as he returned from the mini bar and sat down next to me on the bed in our Las Vegas hotel room.

"If I didn't know any better, I'd think you were trying to control how much I drink. You sure you want to go down that road?" he said, never taking his eyes off the TV.

"It just seems like a lot, is all."

"I just got married. It's time to celebrate. Why don't you loosen up a little bit and try not to piss me off."

In the weeks after returning home from our wedding weekend in Las Vegas, I began to find bottles hidden all over the apartment. For him to demand that I clean the house into a sterile environment and still think he could hide bottles was crazy: I found them in the dirty clothes, in the corners of cabinets, under the bed. When I questioned him, he would tell me that he was trying to deal with the stress of holding down a job and dealing with a fucked-up, lousy wife. Not long after, I found a couple of 6-packs in the fridge as if he had gotten tired of drinking in the shadows. He looked at me as if to say, *Just try and make a big deal out of this.* I decided that I better keep my mouth shut.

In the meantime, Trent was coming home later and later and drunker and drunker. I knew where this was heading: Trent's heart was a smoldering fire that he was dousing with bottles of gasoline. He would walk in and quickly make an assault on my home-making skills, after which, it would begin. He would stumble around the apartment in a state of fury. It was like sharing a house with an agitated, just-gored bull. His mouth would run all night with me as the one and only subject.

"Fucking bitch can't clean a house. Dirt every fucking place I look. She thinks she can get away with this? With my boy? I don't think so, dumb bitch!"

There were no more conversations. There were no spare moments to sit and read or watch TV. All I was allowed to do was tend to Rory, clean, cook or study throughout the evening while Trent sat at the table, beer in hand and talk to the walls about how utterly stupid I was and how he knew I was planning to find someone to have sex with.

I suppose he didn't really need a specific infraction on my part over which to erupt and spill the remaining, ugly contents of his heart, but I sure gave him one. It was one afternoon when I took Rory to some nearby swings. Trent saw us as he was coming home from work. He stopped his car, got out and began walking, a bit unbalanced, over to where we were.

Oh, shit.

"What are you doing out here?" he called out.

"I just wanted to take Rory out for some fresh air, is all. We've only been out here a few minutes and I'm going to take him home in just a moment."

"You've got a lot of work to do to be out here playing around."

"Okay. I can take him back now," I said, frightened. As I lifted Rory from the kiddy swing, his shoe got caught, and I pulled his body, trying to loosen his foot. His head hit against the pole and Rory screamed. And that's when it happened.

"You fucking idiot!" he said. With a blinding right hand, he slapped my face and nearly spun me around. "Nobody is going to hurt my child!"

I couldn't believe he had slapped me while I was still holding Rory. "What are you doing?" I screamed at him.

"Get home right now and give me my child before you kill him!" Trent ripped Rory from my arms, shoved me to the ground and stormed off to his car. He opened the driver's-side door, put Rory on his lap and held him there as he drove around the block to our apartment. I ran home in tears, pushing an empty stroller. When I got inside, Trent was waiting there, seething. I shut the door and leaned my back against it. "He's okay, right?" I asked.

He walked briskly in my direction and without saying a word, he raised his right knee to his chest. With all the spring-loaded fury of a bucking horse, he drove his foot into my chest. I flew back and nearly cracked the door with my body and head. It was at that moment all his demons loudly flapped their wings and flew in a circle around him, filling the air like black crows blocking the sun. Before I could fully crumble to the ground, he drove his right fist into my breast and dug his left fist into my side. I hit the floor with only enough air to produce a breathy squeal. He kicked me in the ribs, hip, and all up and down my legs. He spit in my hair. He stomped my shoulder and back. He pulled my hair and then snapped my earring through my earlobe, blood dripping onto the carpet. He climbed on my back and squeezed the back of my neck and forced my face into the ground, smashing my nose. I could hear something crack.

"Don't ever hurt my child again, do you understand me? If you ever hurt him again I will kill you!" He walked over to the kitchen, opened up the refrigerator, pulled out a beer and sat down at the table breathing heavily.

"Fucking bitch! That's *my* boy. No fucking bitch is ever going hurt my boy. Isn't that right, Jessica? You hear me now, right, you idiot?"

I lay there for a while, as he drank and talked to the walls. The talking, the drinking echoed in my ears and multiplied as if I were lying on the floor of a great cathedral. I got up, got oriented and began to gingerly walk to the bathroom. As I did, I heard him speak. "Yeah, there you go. Get on your feet, bitch. You got some cleaning to do and a shitty dinner to make. I don't think you got time to be hanging out in the park with all you got to do, you dumb fuck!"

I softly closed the door and flipped on the light. I looked in the mirror. Along with tears streaming down my face and snot coming from my nose, crimson red blood was running into my mouth. My earlobe was split into two with a trail of blood coming down my jaw line. I opened my blouse and looked at the red, fist-sized bump on my chest and partially on my breast. I sat down and began to wipe my face clean with a washcloth.

"Jessica! Get out here, dumb fuck. You still got work to do. Your night isn't over."

Over the next year and a half, Trent's demons made permanent residence in our apartment. I was beaten nearly every night for infractions that existed only in Trent's imagination. I was battered so consistently, my torso, starting at my neck, was like a canvas for different shapes of ever-changing black and blue and occasional, transitional yellow. The bruising reached down to my crotch and to the insides of my legs caused by repeated, jackhammer rape. There were welts on my back as well as handprints from slaps. My head had bumps and bruising on my scalp due to his tendency to grab me and push my head into the nearest wall. The incident on the couch after the girls' night out with Carly and Diane became a common occurrence. He kept me up many nights—all night, by pulling me off the bed or couch by my hair. Choking was a favorite; out of the blue he would attack me, and with his hand around my neck, bounce my head against the floor and spit in my face. When he would push me onto the bed or ground and straddle me, he would hold me there with his full weight. When I would try to move, he would restrict me so that I was gasping for breath.

For all his insanity, there was something strangely specific about his torture. He could see how close Rory and I were to each other, so he used him to get to me. "If he drops one more Cheerio, I'm going to beat your ass!" he would scream. "If he drops one more drip of milk onto the carpet, I'm going to beat your ass!" "If any food falls from his high chair, I'm going to beat your ass!" I was chasing Rory around the apartment like a crazy person to make sure nothing he dropped touched the floor. Trent kept one eye on the TV and one eye on Rory. "He better not, dumb shit!"

"Here, honey, let mommy help you with that," I would plead with Rory. If only he knew mommy was trying to save her own life. When Rory would drop something—which was inevitable, considering he was a baby, Trent would beat me. Later during the night, he would rush me, throw me down, tear my clothes off and rape me. I knew the more I fought back, the worse it would get, and the more pain I would have to endure.

The night before Rory's birthday party, Trent beat me horribly for having a conversation with a lady who had walked by our apartment with her toddler. I called to her from our screen door and asked if she knew of any mothers groups. It was a ruse; I knew I'd never be allowed to do anything like meet up with other moms and their kids outside of our apartment. I really just wanted to talk to somebody, even just for a second, if only to exchange a few meaningless pleasantries that could allow me to enjoy the illusion of living like a normal, happy, young mother. But when Trent heard me, he screamed so violently, it startled her. She hurried away. Trent then slammed the door and pulled me back from the doorway. He beat me so badly I vomited on our entryway tile.

Later that day, he told me I smelled like shit and that I needed to clean up. I was taking a bath, and when I stepped out, I stood before the mirror and looked at my bruises. *That son of a bitch*, I said to myself. *He knows exactly what he's doing.* He had been beating me no higher than the top of my neck, leaving my face untouched. He knew bruises on my face would invite questions from anyone who might see me.

The next day we went to a park to meet Trent's parents and family for Rory's birthday party. It was a scorching September afternoon in San Diego. When we arrived, everybody was dressed in the lightest clothes possible. There were hand-held fans, wide-brimmed hats, blow-up pools and buckets of ice. I wore the only thing I had that would cover bruises from the top of my neck on down to my wrists: a black, wool, turtleneck, long-sleeve sweater.

Several of the ladies asked if they could run home to get me something cool to wear. "No, that's okay," I said with sweat streaming down my face and my body drenched. "I'm good. Really. I'm not that hot." I thought I was going to pass out.

Over the next months, Trent started to delineate between my crimes. He saw house-related infractions as deserving of beating and rape. But I began to notice that mistakes I made when talking to men deserved a different kind of punishment: sodomy. If I stayed longer than 30 seconds when delivering rent to the apartment manager, if I sounded too chatty on the phone with the gas and electric guy, if I took too long at the store where there were male cashiers, I was sodomized. When Trent came after me screaming about how I was trying to "fuck other men," I knew what that meant. I grabbed for the pillows to shove in my mouth immediately. There was no way I wanted the neighbors to hear me scream. That would cause trouble. Then my beatings would get worse.

And yet, Trent found a way to make the ultimate punishment seem like child's play. Many mornings I would wake up choking violently as Trent would force his erect penis into my mouth and down my throat. "You're all over town looking for dick when this is what you've got at home? Huh, you dumb bitch?" That Rory would wake up crying and reaching for me as Trent pinned my head down with his pelvis was of no concern to Trent. I could hear Rory scream as I was being suffocated and thinking I would die at any moment. Finally, Trent would pull himself from my mouth and I would cough violently as I rushed to Rory. "Daddy is just playing with mommy, sweetie. Everything is okay!" I would tell him as I cried. *We're killing our baby!* I kept thinking to myself.

I had thought Trent had found the ultimate torture, but there was one more to go. Trent could see that Rory and I clung together every chance we could. When Rory would cry and then reach for me, Trent would pick him up and disallow me from taking him. My little boy would scream and reach his tiny fingers as far as they could go, and Trent would punch or shove me away. "Get out of here, bitch. He doesn't need you!"

There was seemingly nothing on this earth that could hurt more than that. Not the beating, the hair pulling, the suffocating, the rape, sodomy or choking. All of it I would have gladly agreed to so that I would never have to hear and see Rory reach for me and be kept just inches from my grasp. I would fall to my knees and burst into a wail I had no idea I was capable of producing. Trent was pulling my soul apart.

"Look at mommy. Bad mommy. She's all fucked in the head."

Soon, my personality began to close down. I began to assume a defensive posture. I started to turn in. I rarely talked anymore. I never turned on the TV or radio during the days. I worked voraciously. I shooed away salesmen. I kept the curtains closed. I mumbled at times. "Have to work harder. Can't find any dirt. Have to work harder." I went to the post office or store and didn't talk to a soul. I rushed to get home. I looked in the mirror. A zombie looked back.

When Trent was yelling at me, I put my head down and stared at the ground. When he beat me, I cried but rarely made a sound. When he had sex with me, I stared at the ceiling. When he knocked food to the ground. I simply picked it back up.

About two weeks after I missed my period, I took a test. It was positive. I went directly to the women's center the first chance I had and had an abortion. I didn't even think twice. I don't think I had the capacity to think twice. My mind was working off survival instincts. There was no room for a baby or even consideration of it. I was not about to bring another baby into my world.

Some nights, every great once in a while, he would come home and be in a loving mood. He would apologize and tell me how wonderful I really was. "You're so beautiful, Jessica. You're such a good person. You don't deserve any of this. I love you so much." I would collapse into his arms like a person who had been pulled from a frigid river, gasping for air. Tears would stream down my face, and I could barely control myself, trembling and clutching at his shirt. I was in so much pain, so depleted, that even my brutal captor, with a kind word, had the power to reduce me into a heap of sobbing gratitude.

It created in me a new anxiety, one where I didn't know what to expect that night when Trent came home. I would have rather known I was going to get beaten. I knew how to deal with that.

About this time, my mom started to call more frequently, which I was overjoyed about, and the issue that we fought over in the restaurant was long over and fully accepted. I think instinctively, she knew that I was in need of her voice on the other end of the line, even if all we chatted about was Rory or clothes or hair. Each word went past my ears and straight to my soul. It wasn't what she was saying, it was *that* she was saying. She was my connection to the outside world, sanity and any semblance of love.

One day she called excited to tell me about an idea that she had. She offered to pay for daycare so I could finish up my sociology degree without having to keep navigating Trent's constantly changing work schedule or call upon the elderly lady down the hall. Grateful for my mom's gift, I took her up on it. Of course, I said very little about it to Trent. Too much information, and things could go very wrong.

Terri, the woman who ran the day care where I took Rory, had big wooden lockers where she stored each child's belongings. After about a month of taking Rory to her, and just one day after I had taken a particularly brutal beating from Trent, I was standing by the wooden lockers while waiting to pick up Rory when I got a strange feeling. I was drawn to the lockers and didn't know why. I looked at them again and rubbed my hand across the polished wood. Like a thought that my mind was desperately struggling to create, perhaps as an act of self-preservation, it came to me—an idea. I asked her if I could keep a bag inside Rory's locker that was to be just for me if I ever needed it. She gave me a quizzical look. "Well...sure," she replied.

A week later, when I was at school, Helen, a woman from my sociology class whom I had been paired with for a project, looked into my eyes while we stood talking. From the odd look on her face, I knew she could tell something wasn't quite right with me. She began to ask questions. At first I felt defensive, but her warmth suddenly looked like an opportunity. The same strange feeling that pulsed through my body when I saw the wooden lockers at the day care center was back. "Let me ask you something," I said.

"Sure. Anything," Helen offered.

"If I'm ever in trouble one day, would you allow me to come and stay at your house—just for a time, if I ever really needed it?"

"Well, what's going on?"

"It's really more than I can explain right now." I looked around our classroom to see if anybody happened to be looking. I pulled up the sleeve of my sweatshirt to the middle of my forearm. A bruise in the shape of a hand was revealed. Helen's eyes widened.

"So can I?" I asked her. She looked at me with shock in her face.

"Anytime you need, you just come over," she said.

A few weeks later, my mom offered to come over to our apartment, to see Rory and help me do the taxes. She noticed that for the two hours that she was there, I had hardly spoken a thing, and I certainly wasn't acting like my old self.

"Do you and Trent want to come over for dinner tonight?" mom asked.

"No. Thanks," I told her without a hint of gratitude. "We can't," I said.

I walked her to the door and she gave Rory a kiss and a squeeze. She looked at my face again, gaunt and lifeless. "Well, okay," she said looking harder at me than I felt comfortable with. "Goodbye."

As I shut and locked the door and began to walk away, I heard her knock again. I opened the door. "Are you sure you're okay, honey?" she asked, trying to see deep inside me.

I looked at my mom for a moment. "I'm fine, mom. Really."

"You don't look fine. And you don't act fine. Is something the matter?"

"The matter, what—no. I mean, I'm just tired, is all. We're fine, I mean I'm fine."

I stepped closer. "Look…" I said quietly. Suddenly I thought better of it than to finish that sentence. I gave her an intense look in the eye and shook my head as if to say, *Not now. Go away.*

She got the hint. "Okay, sweetie," she said.

"I'll talk to you later," I said as I closed the door and locked it again.

"What the fuck!" I heard Trent yell from the living area that was a level higher than the entryway. He came to the railing. "What the fuck!" he said again. I looked at him and leaned against the door and just stared back. My eyes must have said, *I really don't want to deal with your garbage right now, whatever it is.*

"You mother fucker!" he yelled. With a single leap, he jumped down to where I stood with Rory in my arms. He took a swing at me and missed, hitting Rory in the face and splitting open his lip. Rory screamed. I screamed.

Trent yanked Rory from my arms, dropped him to the side and began to pummel me to the ground with all his weight behind powerful rights and lefts that left me gasping for the air to be able to cry out.

"Don't you ever let my business come out your mouth, do you understand me, you stupid cunt?"

Trent walked away from me, right past Rory, who was sending blood-curdling screams of his own into the sky. I pulled myself onto my elbows and looked around in a daze. I reached for Rory, whose lips were curled down from crying, exposing a giant cut and lots of blood. I picked him up and ran into the small bathroom just off our entryway. When I flipped on the lights and saw the blood pouring from his mouth and the terror in his face, I knew that was it. I had seen enough. Trent had made our home a hell. There was no way Rory should have to live this way. Adrenaline fired off in my body like it was being injected into my veins. I started to frantically put water on his lips and a washcloth on his face to cool him down. We were in there for about five minutes, with my heart pumping so rapidly I was short of breath. I knew I had reached a precipice. Rory's cry started to subside as we looked in the mirror together, two tragic faces looking at each other. Finally, I opened the door as quietly as I could. I stepped out with Rory on my hip and took my purse from an area table near the entryway, opened the front door, and ran as fast as my tortured body could take me.

Out there, somewhere, was a baby bag, a classmate who would let me stay with her, and hopefully, if I could run fast enough, freedom.

∞∞∞

So you were living this life and still going to school?
Yup.
Did you ever think about quitting? I mean, you had a lot on your mind.
No. I think school saved my life in a way.
So when did you do your homework—between beatings?
And feedings and cleaning.
What were you going to do with your degree?
Become a social worker.
You mean, after all you were going through, you were still preparing to walk into the pain of dysfunctional families? What attracted you to that?
I think I don't like it when people are lonely.
That's how you see people in dysfunctional families. Lonely?
Pain is always lonely.

11
NIBBLING AT THE HEELS

THE SOUND OF MY OWN SHOES clicking against the pavement as I ran with Rory on my hip felt unbearably slow, especially with my heart racing 10 times the pace of my feet, and there was still another 50 yards to go before I reached my car.

Shit! Shit! Shit!

Rory was still screaming as I finally reached my car door, opened it, and roughly tossed him in his car seat without buckling him in. I backed out of our space expecting that I would see Trent in my rear-view mirror jumping on the trunk at any moment. As I scanned left and right, I didn't see him.

I screeched out of the complex without any idea where I was going to drive first. I turned left down a side street and gunned my car toward the main avenue, my eyes darting back and forth between the road and my mirror. Just then, 150 yards back, I saw Trent's car come around the corner and onto the street with an angry screech and growl.

I pushed harder on the gas pedal and flew down the two-lane street. A sedan driven by an elderly man pulled onto the street right behind me. A red light was just ahead and I ran it, turning right. The elderly man stopped at the corner and calmly waited for an opening in cross traffic as Trent skidded up behind him and laid on the horn. He now found himself blocked by the old guy and a Corvette waiting to go straight.

I tore down the main avenue. My first thought was to pull into any parking lot and try to hide in a space. I nearly turned into one but then changed my mind—if he happened to see me, I'd be pinned in and caught immediately. I roared south into the heavily Vietnamese part of town and saw Trent's car barreling after me in my rear-view mirror.

I shot through a yellow light at Balboa Avenue and, as I looked behind me, I could see Trent got stuck when the light turned red and heavy cross traffic blocked his way. Even so, I knew my running was over. There was no way I was going to endanger Rory by going on a high-speed chase all over Mira Mesa. I looked for a place to pull into where the avenue begins to wind left. With any luck he wouldn't be able to see what I did next.

I turned into a small, busy strip mall with a couple of Vietnamese restaurants, two shops, a market and a taco shop. I found a parking spot and pulled in and turned off the motor. I looked around for a moment, Rory still filling the car with screams. I didn't tend to him, not yet—all I could do was keep scanning the road, side to side, breathing so heavily I nearly choked with each gasp. Quickly, I started the car, backed out, and then backed into the space again, this time with the nose out in case I needed to peel out of there. I turned off the car.

I turned around and pushed Rory's bottom deep into the seat and buckled him in as his arms reached for me. I held his hand, "Honey, mommy's right here. You have to stay in your seat, okay, sweetie?

Everything's going to be okay. Now, please stop crying! Shhh, shhh, shhh."

I didn't see Trent. I began to weigh my options. He could have passed the strip mall and would be well down the road, looking for me. He could be racing toward the 15 Freeway to try to prevent me from getting on and going to my mom's house. He could be swinging back around and trying to cut me off from getting on the 805 Freeway from Balboa. Or will he look for me here? Is the same reason I chose this strip mall the same reason he would suspect it?

I sat in the car, holding Rory's hand and looking out the back window toward the street. I took notice of the stores, who went in and what was on the other side of the doors. I chose which store I would run into if I needed to. I watched. I waited. I looked at my watch. An hour had passed and I was still with my knees on my seat looking out the back window. I looked at my watch again. I had another problem. Terri, the woman at the day care, ended her day at 6 o'clock, and it was fast approaching. I would have to get back on the road and make my way to her, just three miles away. But I wouldn't be able to wait for cover of nightfall to do it. Even though dusk was approaching, there was still plenty of light. I waited until the last moment: 5:45. I started up my car. Rory wasn't screaming any more but was visibly miserable, fussing under the pain of having a dirty diaper and nothing to eat for hours. I turned onto the street and entered what felt like shark-infested waters. I drove toward the day care, which was a house in the neighborhood just west of ours.

Trent had never been there, so I knew there was no way he would suspect the route. Even so, I kept an eye out. After a few minutes of head-on-a-swivel driving, I pulled up to the small white house with a chain link fence around the property and balls and play things in the front yard. I took Rory from his seat and charged to the front door and opened it without knocking. Terri was inside with a few kids left to be picked up and a young lady she employed as a helper.

"Hi Terri," I said without even a hint of pleasantry. "I'm here to get my bag out of Rory's locker." Besides being a disheveled mess, she could see I was deadly serious.

"Go right ahead," she said standing back from me like I was radioactive. She used her arm to wave me into action.

"I need to change him, too."

"Change him, no problem," she quickly said.

I grabbed my bag, changed Rory and shoveled some applesauce down his throat that I had stored inside his bag. I stood up and thanked Terri.

"Take these," she said, offering more jars of food. I went to the window and peered out to see if I could spot Trent's car. I didn't see anything.

"Thanks again," I said as I headed out the door. I suppose I could have stayed there, but I didn't want to take the chance that if Trent was rolling through the neighborhoods behind where we lived, he might see my car and then terrorize Terri and the other kids. Besides, Terri's was much too close to where we lived, and Helen lived nearly 20 miles away. I would be safer there—Trent wouldn't have a clue where I was.

By then it was dark enough for headlights. I made my way out of the neighborhood, then jumped on the freeway going north, took the crosstown freeway going east, then onto the 15 Freeway going south just to pick the most indirect route I could think of. I kept the radio off while I drove; I wanted to stay alert so I could scan every car that passed. I kept to the speed limit. I didn't want anything to do with cops and whatever system they would force me through as a battered wife. I thought of the hell I had just endured. I thought of Trent going back and forth on the streets, and then back to the apartment to check for me. I thought about what he'd do to me if he ever found me. I felt scared. I felt sad for my son. I felt like I was nibbling at the heels of death.

I felt proud that I was standing up.

I arrived at Helen's place, a small apartment on an out-of-the-way street on a hill in El Cajon, and I prayed that she was there. I grabbed Rory from his car seat while he was sleeping and ran up the stairs to her apartment, #207. I knocked with all the urgency that I was telling myself I shouldn't so I wouldn't scare her. I couldn't help it.

"Who is it?" came Helen's concerned voice from inside.

"It's Jessica. Jessica Yaffa!"

She opened the door with a burst and looked at me. "Come in," she said. I quickly walked in, and before she could even close the door, tears erupted from my eyes, and I collapsed in her arms.

I was safe.

12

TO THE END OF
THE MALL

"HELLO?"

"Mom, it's me!" I screamed into the phone.

"Jessica!" my mom said frantically. "Are you okay?"

"Mom, it's 10 o'clock at night. Where have you been?"

"Here! I've been here all night. Where are you?"

"Well, why haven't you been answering your phone?" I demanded.

"Because Trent has been calling me every 15 minutes ever since you ran away. Where are you?"

"I'm with a friend. I don't think I'm going to tell you where I am because I don't want Trent pestering you to tell him. When he asks, just tell him I didn't tell you for just that reason."

"Well, are you okay? Is Rory okay?"

"He's fine. He's asleep. I'm okay—freaked out but okay." It occurred to me that while my mom listened, she probably figured that I was on the run because of a particularly bad fight, one where Trent got physical with me. Considering that I had never let her in on the brutality of my life, even going so far as rarely bringing Trent to her house and always avoiding seeing her when I was visibly bruised, I knew her mind could only imagine a one-thousandth of what was really happening.

"Thank God," she said. "I have been worried out of my mind."

"I know, mom, I know. I'm so sorry."

She asked what I was going to do next. I sat there on Helen's kitchen stool in the pink bathrobe and pajamas Helen provided for me. I moved out of the way of her kitchen window—just in case.

"I have no idea," I said. I looked around the room as if an answer might come. "I really have no idea what I'm going to do."

Over the next several days, Trent called my mother at a frantic pace, just as she said, nearly every 15 minutes until late into the night and then starting again first thing in the morning. It was hell for her. Every time my mom decided to answer, Trent was crying and nearly coming apart. Mom knew to stay out of the fray when Trent would try to bait her into talking about what was going on between him and me. "Sorry. I know nothing, and I want to know nothing," she'd say.

More than anything, he cried about how much he missed Rory and how he didn't think it was fair that all of a sudden, his beloved boy was whisked from his life. He was going out of his mind as he thought of his son out there, somewhere, with no idea of his whereabouts. It wasn't right, he'd say. No man should be unaware of where his boy is.

Helen was single and more than gracious about sharing her tiny one-bedroom. She made it clear that she didn't want me to feel pressured to tell her my immediate plans or when I might be leaving. I didn't know that is what I needed to hear—I didn't know much of anything at that moment—but it seemed like there was simply nothing she wanted from me even though I had just invaded her life. It felt so good that I wanted her to keep talking. I engaged her in conversation every chance I could because everything she said *didn't* have any responsibility attached. In fact, she took the next day off work to be with me, tend to my bruises, and be there as a little bit of reassurance that I was safe. She played with Rory and asked me to just sit and "detox" from all that I had been through. "Cry, scream, throw a fit. It's all okay," she said. When I broke down and cried on her couch, she came close, brought me tissues and stroked my hair. "Let it out, and don't be afraid," she said. "You're stronger than I could ever be."

The first night, she opened her refrigerator to see what she had to feed us and didn't see much. "Hmm," she said. "Not good."

"Helen," I said. "I don't care what you have, whatever it is, it's fine." I just didn't want her to leave.

She lovingly put sheets on her couch for me and gave me a quilted blanket that her grandmother had made for her. She turned the lights off with me tucked in like a little girl. Rory was sleeping soundly, and I was comfortable and warm and cared for. Even so, as I lay there in the dark with silence all around me, I could feel the pulse of fear going through my body. I was dead tired, and yet my eyes darted around the ceiling. I looked at her front door. There was no way, absolutely no way Trent could have any idea where we were. I searched my mind again for any possibility. No, there was no possibility. I was safe. It was a done deal. We were both safe.

Even so, I got up, grabbed her kitchen-table chair and wedged it underneath the handle of the front door.

On the morning of the third day, I called my mom. "I know he's driving you crazy, mom. I'm so sorry I brought this into your life," I told her.

"I'm just going to tell you what he wants me to tell you, okay? This is not me, it's him, alright?" mom said.

"You're going to relay a message to me from him?" I asked. "I don't even want to hear it," I snapped.

"Just let me tell you so that I can tell him I did tell you, okay? Because he's going to pressure me about it."

"What is it?"

"He wants you to know that he respects what you've done and that he knows he's been bad to you, but he wants to see Rory because he's going crazy not being able to hold him. He says he absolutely will not touch you and he's not interested in you. He just wants to be with his boy." He was obviously laying it on pretty thick.

"That's crazy. It isn't going to happen," I told her. "I mean, you wouldn't do it, would you?"

"It's your call."

"Wait a minute—that's not a 'no'!"

"Because it's not my life."

"Yeah, but it sounds like you'd consider it. I'm not going to see that lunatic."

"Well, you should hear him. He doesn't sound like a lunatic."

"What do you mean?"

"Well, at first he was frantic, but now he sounds totally reasonable and sensible—and very apologetic. He knows what he did and he's really sorry about it. He just wants to see Rory is all. I mean it's really killing him."

I sat silently on Helen's green couch, my elbow on the arm and my hand on my forehead. I wanted to finally launch into all the horrors my mom didn't know about—the torture, the torment, the constant verbal lashings, the nightly rapes, the endless fists—but I couldn't. Hadn't she put two and two together so I didn't have to go there? I opened my mouth again to speak. A cascade of violence flooded my mind, and as it did, it felt so oppressive I couldn't move. I just wasn't prepared to step back into my nightmare and I knew I could never dent the truth of my experience. I could only fail and I just didn't have the wherewithal to fail. "I'm tired, mom," I said, and I got off the phone.

I sat on Helen's couch for a half hour thinking about it. I wondered if I was making the right decision to keep my son away from his father. I knew the pain of wanting your daddy.

I had decided to call the lawyer that Helen had given me the name of, and in our 15-minute consultation, he talked about things like restraining orders, temporary custody and legal separation. I wasn't in any kind of condition to wrap my head around stuff like that. I got off the phone, sat there as Rory played with Tupperware around my feet, and thought about what my mom had said.

What should I do? I thought to myself. I was still undecided as I picked up the phone and called Trent at work.

"Security, this is Trent," he said on the phone. A shiver went down my spine.

"This is Jessica. What's your problem?"

"Jessica!"

"Can we just get to it, please?"

"How are you?"

"Never mind that. I want you to stop calling my mom—do you understand me?"

"Look, baby. I know I'm driving her crazy, but you have to understand what I'm going through. If I don't see my son, I don't know what I'm going to do with myself. I feel like part of me is missing, you know?"

"It's called beating your wife."

"I know. I know, and I'm so sorry. I can't tell you how sorry I am that I did that to you. That will never happen again. I will never lay a hand on you again."

"Well you're never going to get that chance."

"Look, let's not talk about you and I. All I really want is to see Rory. We can talk about us later, or never. Whatever. I just have to know—how is he doing?"

"Fine. His lip hurts."

"You see? Right there! Can't you see how I feel? I just have to hold my boy and tell him how sorry daddy is. I have to, baby—a man has to make amends with his son when he hurts him like that. Please!"

I sat there cold for a moment. "You should have thought about that a long time ago."

"Well, I'm thinking about it now and that's all I have. You just have to let a man do right by his son. He needs me too, you know! Please, Jessica. Please let me apologize to my boy."

I gave him the silent treatment.

"Listen," he said, "I know you're afraid of me. I can understand that. But if you'll meet me, you'll see I mean you no harm. We can meet in a busy place and everything—so you can feel as safe as possible. Just let me see my boy. Please!"

I felt myself giving in. It wasn't much, but it was there, a little slight feeling that my resolve, once again, had grown soft.

"Where do you want to meet?"

Trent asked to meet in the front of a drug store in a busy strip mall near our apartment in Mira Mesa. I knew it well. It was always full of people and well lit. I told him I'd do it and that he had exactly a half hour with Rory. At exactly 30 minutes, I was leaving.

"Fine, that's fine," Trent said. "That's all I want. I can't thank you enough!"

"Trent!" I said before getting off the phone. "If I get a slight whiff of beer from you, I'm out of there, no questions asked."

"No problem. Bye! Thanks!" he said, and hung up.

I went over on unsteady legs to where Rory was playing and picked him up. "You want to see daddy, honey?" I asked him. I kissed him and held him close. I put him back down. *Dear God, what am I doing?* I thought to myself.

Helen came home around 3 p.m. and I asked her to sit down.

"I feel the need to let Trent see Rory," I told her.

"Uh huh," Helen replied.

"So, that's what I'm going to do."

"How are you going to do that?"

"I'm going to take Rory to him."

"*You're* going to do it?" she said with shock.

"Yeah."

"I'm absolutely opposed to that. Not that it matters what I think, but I think this is a very bad idea," she said sternly.

"I understand why you would think that, but I think everything will calm down a little if I just let him see Rory for a few minutes."

She looked at me and shook her head in disbelief. "Have you made up your mind?" she asked.

"Yes."

"Are you going alone?"

"Just me and Rory."

"I am fully against you going, but I am not letting you go alone. I'm going with you."

I was going to ask her anyway.

It was around 6 o'clock and almost dark. Helen drove her car and was too mad to even talk. I sat in the back with Rory, who was in his seat. I talked playfully with Rory to help keep him occupied, but my heart was thumping. I could feel that my shirt was wet and my hands were clammy. When we pulled into the strip mall, I pointed the way. As I looked, I saw Trent standing in front of the drug store, stuffed bear in hand.

Helen parked the car and I moved to get Rory out of his seat. I got out of the car holding Rory and we walked the 20 yards to where Trent was waiting. Trent held out the bear and shook it as we approached. "Look, Rory. Look what daddy brought you!" he said like nothing was wrong. He took Rory from my arms, and Rory squirmed violently and then reached for me.

"It's okay, honey," I said. "Give daddy kisses."

Trent leaned forward to give me a hug. I stiffened and pulled back.

"Alright, okay," he said. "No problem." He looked at the car. "Who's she?"

I looked back at Helen, who was watching us. "A friend. No names, Trent."

He held Rory and kissed and caressed him. Rory seemed to be a bit confused by the whole thing. Still, Trent was enlivened by the chance to hold Rory. "Daddy missed his big boy," he told him. "Did Rory miss daddy?"

They played and cuddled together for about five minutes, with Trent talking about the bear and how much daddy missed Rory. They seemed to be doing fine together. *So far, so good,* I thought. Just then, Trent turned to me and said, "Hey, can we just go for a walk and talk a bit?"

"Why?"

"Well I'd rather not just stand here in front of these doors the whole time being watched by some woman I don't know. Come with us and let me have the chance to give you a few of my thoughts about how sorry I am all this happened."

"Where are we going?"

"We'll just, I don't know, walk to the end of the mall and back, okay? We'll take it slow and easy."

I looked back at Helen, who was still watching unwaveringly. "Just a minute," I said to Trent.

I took Rory back from Trent and walked over to Helen. She looked at me as if to say, "You're done? Great!"

"He wants to go for a walk," I said to her as I approached.

She looked a little pained. "You're not going to do it, are you?"

"He says he just wants to tell me how sorry he is without you watching. I think it will be okay. As soon as we get back, we're out of here."

"This is a bad idea," she said with conviction.

"I think we'll be alright. Look, if we're not back in 10 minutes, call the cops," I told her. I turned to walk back to Trent. "Just to the end and back," I called to him.

"Yup," he said.

As the three of us walked, Trent held Rory in his arms and began to tell me just how sorry he was that it had come to this. I wasn't particularly interested. I just wanted to get this little jaunt out of the way so I could get back in the car and go back to Helen's.

We came to the end of the strip mall and Trent was still talking. He was getting pretty animated, as if he were excited about something and feeling good. "Oh, hey," he said with a glint in his eyes. "Look at this. I want to show you something." He motioned for me to follow.

"What?" I said curtly.

"It's just that," he said as he pointed.

"I don't see what you're pointing at."

"Just come here. You'll see it better," he insisted, taking hold of my arm with his wide hand and clamping down. My breathing immediately began to shorten and I felt myself make a succession of quick gasps. He yanked my arm and pulled me over to his car, which was parked just around the corner of the mall and just out of sight of Helen. He opened the door and pointed inside. A gun lay on the passenger's seat.

"Get inside the car and keep your mouth shut," he said through clenched teeth. "If you don't, I'm going to fucking blow your brains out!"

∞∞∞∞

What were the signs I should have been looking for?
    For what?
So that I could have known it was going to go bad.
    Oh. I think he was the sign.
So you think I should have known the whole time?
    No blame game, Jessica. It doesn't do you any good and really. it doesn't apply.

Let me ask you this: Did you know early on in the story that something dangerous was going to happen when I showed up?

Not necessarily by anything he specifically said. However, later on, there was something he *didn't* say that was a red flag.

What was that?

He never apologized to Rory.

13

THE BEST PLACE
FOR A MURDER

I JUST STOOD THERE.

"Get the fuck in the car!" he growled.

I looked at the corner of the building that blocked the sightline between Helen and us. My hope was that Helen had seen us disappear behind the building and surely would be rushing over to us at any moment.

"Did you hear me?" he said as he gave me a good shake. I continued to stall. "Do you know how fucking close I am to ripping the hair out of your head?"

"Please, Trent, let's not do this."

"I ain't here to talk things over," he snarled. "Now get in the car!" he said once more, only this time, he shoved my arm up against my body, and I hit the edge of the roof of his car. It hurt.

I looked toward the street once more but didn't see Helen. There was no one walking nearby to scream out to. I got in the driver's side like he told me. *"C'mon, Helen,"* I whispered to myself.

Later I learned that Helen had done exactly what I thought she might. She got out of her car and ran to where she could see around the side of the building but saw nothing. When I got into the car and Trent got in the back seat with Rory on his lap, we were already out of sight.

"Drive, bitch!" Trent said, reaching over the seat and plunging the key into the ignition and turning it over. He pushed the barrel of the pistol into the nape of my neck.

I immediately felt like the stupidest girl in the world. I took a deep breath. I put the car in drive and slowly nudged the gas. "Where we going?" I said haltingly. I made sure that my maneuvering out of the parking space took as long as possible. For a moment, there was a vestige of hope born out of the last three days away from Trent, and I felt myself believe. I believed that we were not going to get onto the road, that Helen would appear and rap on the window or the cops that I was sure she had called would screech to a halt in front of us. I looked in the rearview mirror. I could see Rory's sad eyes as he sat on Trent's lap. *He's going to be okay,* I thought to myself. *He will. He'll see.*

As we inched toward the edge of the parking lot, I saw that no one was coming to save us. A black sedan with dark-tinted windows slowly drove in the cross traffic in front of me, left to right. As it passed, I could see that it was not a police car, which should have been abundantly clear from the outset, and I felt that little ray of hope inside my body pass out of sight right along with it. I couldn't believe it. Rory and I were in the car with Trent and completely at his mercy.

"This is going to be real cut and dry, Jessica. You take me over to the dude's house you've been staying with, and when I see him, I go over there, put this fucking gun to his head and then rip a hole in his skull. Then, I put it against your head and blow your brains out all over him. Think I'm kidding? I got a fucking hard-on to do it—I can't wait! Now drive!"

"The woman you saw in the car, that's who I stayed with," I pleaded.

"Bullshit, girl. You think I'm going to fall for that? What do you think I am?"

"I swear I'm telling the truth. I know her from class, and she said I could stay with her if I ever needed to, so that's what I did!"

"Tell you what then," he said with mock sincerity. "Drive over to the house you were staying at. You're going to go up to her door and if she doesn't come out, then I'll know you been fucking some dude, and then you're dead."

"Well, of course she's not there. She's in the car in the parking lot! You just saw her!"

He pushed the gun into the bottom of my skull tipping my head forward. "Just drive! You better hope she's there, bitch."

"I don't under—"

"Shut up and drive!"

I'm as good as dead! I thought to myself. *This asshole is crazy enough to do it and there's no way Helen's there.* I immediately began to search around in my mind for other places that I could drive rather than show up at Helen's, who I had last seen sitting in her car 80 yards away. I had to drive somewhere. Not at all sure what I should do, I drove slowly in the direction of Helen's apartment and just hoped and prayed that somehow she did decide to call the cops—and still raced home.

And then he started. "How many guys you fuck in the last three days, huh? You got a boyfriend out there who's waiting for you now? Bitch has to fuck. Even though she got dick at home, fucking cheating bitch has to fuck."

And so it went, mile after earsplitting mile: Trent barking in my ear and Rory, who was now screaming while on Trent's lap—and a gun inches from his and my face.

The drive to El Cajon was the longest 17 miles of my life. I sobbed the entire way. *What a fool, what a fool I am!* I thought to myself. I even drove my fist into my own thigh—a move violent enough to garner some attention from Trent, but he didn't say anything.

As we drove up to Helen's apartment, Trent told me to park the car under a tree that blocked the light of a nearby lamppost. It was quiet, dark and out of the way. All things considered, it was probably the best place in the lot for a murder.

The car was parked facing Helen's apartment. "Turn off the ignition," Trent said. I turned off the car and we sat still and quiet for a minute or two as we simply looked toward the apartments. I wondered what was next. Suddenly, Trent forced his way over the seats and scrambled to the front passenger seat, leaving Rory in the back. "Go ahead, bitch," he said. "Get out the car."

I turned to Rory who had gone nearly hoarse from crying. "Honey," I said, trying to calm him.

"Shut up and get out the car! He don't need you!" Trent said pushing me away violently. I slowly opened the door and stepped out. Trent climbed over to the driver's seat and immediately shut the door and locked it. He rested his wrists on top of the steering wheel, pointing the gun toward Helen's door.

"Get walking, bitch."

I looked at Rory through the window, who was no longer screaming, just looking longingly at his mommy as if to say, *Aren't you coming to get me?* I turned and made gradual, small steps toward the tiny two-story, white stucco apartment building with my mind whirring, feeling the weight of a gun pointed at my back and trying to figure out what I was going to do when I got to the door.

I heard my shoes make crisp, clearly defined crunching sounds on the downed leaves. My eyes darted around from side to side searching for ideas, any ideas. I kept my head low and my shoulders high, however irrationally, imagining that this scrunched pose could protect me from the shot that might be fired toward the back of my head at any moment. My breathing was short and halting. My heart raced.

I began to climb the stairs still trying to hatch a plan. If I made any move, like run into an apartment or run away, he would still have Rory—and I wasn't going to bet on the chance that he wouldn't kill my son.

As I slowly stepped onto the second floor landing, my eyes were in a frantic search for a solution to my problem. I looked at everything having no idea what I was looking for. Door mats. Railings. Door handles. Apartment numbers. A broom. Suddenly, I noticed there was a clock that was visible through the curtains in apartment #205. The time read 6:41 pm. I stopped. My eyes darted around again. I looked down for a moment. I had to take a chance on Trent's irrationality. Perhaps if I showed him enough conviction in my reason for turning around and going back, then he might give himself the freedom to not completely understand it in order to allow it. It was a small chance, but it was all I had. I quickly turned around and waved to Trent and began running back toward the car—directly toward the barrel of his gun.

Trent pushed his squeaky car door open, stepped outside, and stood with the gun pointing at me. "What are you doing, you dumb bitch?"

"I forgot," I called out rather nonchalantly as I ran. "She's not going to be home until 7 pm. She's on her way. We can wait 20 minutes, right?"

He looked at me quizzically. "Twenty minutes?" he said. "Fuck."

I asked him to let me inside the car. Suddenly everything seemed to go into slow motion.

I saw him look at the inside of his door.

I saw him reach down.

I saw him touch the door panel.

And just like that, I saw him do the unthinkable. He unlocked my door.

I had just bought us 20 minutes to live. As I was getting in, I started thinking about my next move. I looked at Trent, who seemed confused. I looked at Rory, who looked at me with heavy eyes. I knew that what I said and did next would either save his life and mine—or cause us to die. I had to think fast.

"Trent, I know I blew it," I said.

"You fucking blew it, you bitch," he snapped.

"Yup, no doubt," I said.

"Who do you think you are, walking out my house with my son? You thought you were going to get away with that?"

Over the next hour, Trent opened up the depths of his soul, playing just about every character imaginable: from insulted husband to lost little boy to righteous crusader to terrified father to disrespected tough guy to deeply apologetic, regretful, self-pitying loser to gun-wielding demon. By the end, he had worked himself into a state of deep, almost primal loathing: venom was dripping from his mouth as he pushed me up against the corner of the passenger side, gun to my throat. He was screaming so violently his voice was giving way as invective after invective exploded from his mouth.

"Fuck you, mother fucker! Fuck you!" His eyes sprouted two streams of tears down his sweaty cheeks and his nose ran into his mouth. His breath enveloped my face. The veins in his forehead and neck pushed angrily at his skin.

I held my breath and slightly turned my face away. What was next? A shot? A crushing blow to my face from the barrel of his gun?

Suddenly, he furiously backed away from me, got out of the car, went to the trunk and began to open it. *Oh, no,* I thought. *This is it.*

He came back to the car with a six-pack, plopped it between us, pulled one from the plastic, opened it with an ear-piercing *schplitk!* and began to guzzle. His knee started to bounce like a piston and I could feel the car shake. I sat there watching his madness, still pinned up against the corner, afraid to move. He switched the gun to his left hand, threw down the empty can and started up the car hard enough to break it. My eyes opened widely. He put the car in drive, and we drove out of the parking lot and onto the street and headed for our apartment.

All the way home, I didn't make a move, and I didn't make a sound.

14

The Sound of
the Blind

THERE WAS A HORSE that chased a dog. There was a man's face that stared back at me. There was a snake whose tail had claws. There was a woman with a bonnet.

The usual cast of characters that were found in the random squiggly lines on our bedroom ceiling were still there to keep me company as Trent grunted and groaned and surged on top of me. *I think the dog only thinks the horse is chasing him. The horse is actually running from the snake who has scared it with its awful tail. I think the man must be in love with the woman. She keeps part of her face hidden by the bonnet to make her more alluring. She is in love with him, too.*

When he was spent, he rolled over and enjoyed the post-release high, his body heaving up and down like a wounded animal. I got up and began to pull my nightgown from my dresser.

"What're you doing?" Trent asked groggily.

"I'm going to go to take a shower and go to sleep," I replied, touching my cheekbone that was swelling from a slap.

"Like hell. You got a shit load of work to do."

"It's 11 at night. I'll get to it tomorrow," I said. I was furious and embarrassed that I was back in our apartment after nearly succeeding in escaping. It was a brash thing to say. It was playing with fire. But for the moment, I didn't care. He lifted his head to look at me a bit surprised. He put it back down. He was going to let this one slide. After chasing me down and smacking me around when we had gotten home plus his end-of-every-day sexual act, he was just interested in getting some sleep.

He reached into a drawer and grabbed a pen and dragged himself to the kitchen and opened the fridge as I walked toward the bathroom.

When I got out of the shower, Trent had gone to bed and fallen asleep. I slipped into bed next to him. In about four hours, I would learn that my horrible life had just gotten worse.

Three o'clock in the morning was when Rory usually woke up and this night was no different. I got up and walked to the kitchen to get him some juice. As I reached inside the fridge, I looked at the carton and saw that there was a horizontal line of ink about a quarter of the way down. *Hmm*, I thought. *What is that?*

At sunrise, I was up with Rory in the kitchen, sitting him in his high chair, when Trent came around the corner dressed for work. He went to the fridge, took the juice carton and walked to the window. He held the carton up to the light coming from the window and looked through the carton. *My God*, I thought. *Trent drew the line.*

It took me only a few minutes to figure out why. Trent had viewed my attempt at running away not as a desperate woman trying to save her life or get her son out of harm, but as betrayal, as an attempt to cheat with another man. Therefore, his response—which followed its own twisted, darkly paranoid logic—was to batten down the hatches. He put lines on the carton before going to bed so he could tell in the morning whether I did indeed give juice to Rory. If the juice level hadn't moved from where the line was drawn, it meant that the only reason I got up in the middle of the night was to walk outside into the waiting arms of a boyfriend. It was insane.

His paranoia then progressed. He began to get up with me in the middle of the night and follow me as I tended to Rory—just so he could know for sure that I didn't step out of the apartment to give a boy an impassioned kiss and a feel before returning to bed.

He also figured out the mileage from the apartment to every location on his approved list of places where I could drive, including my school, Rory's day care and my mom's house. He would check the odometer in the morning and then again when he got home. Violations were dealt with in blood, bruises and rape.

When it came to going to the grocery store, bank, post office or any of the other places that required a drive, Trent would drive me and then hover close by. I would be in the bank with Trent just outside on the sidewalk looking in at me through the glass doors. Or he would watch me from the wings of the post office as I stepped up to the window for help. Guys were everywhere, as he saw it, and he was there to limit their access to me. Even going down to the mailbox in front of our apartment complex, Trent would walk me down, stop, and let me walk the rest of the way while he watched.

The most chilling of all was when I had to walk to the laundry room at the end of the sidewalk that went along our apartment window. Instead of making the trip with me, he would allow me to walk out the door by myself with the laundry basket in my arms. Then he would go to the window, and I would hear the window blinds click as he would peek through at me, watching each step all the way down to the laundry room. The sound would make my jaw tighten and my pulse race. It wasn't so much that he was watching—he always did that. It was that it wasn't a face. It was two motionless, expressionless eyes. No nose. No chin. Each time I felt the eyes stare at me, whatever dignity I still had seeped from my body.

Once I was in the laundry room, I had two minutes to unload my basket, start the wash and be back in the apartment. It was two minutes to avoid being attacked. It was a ridiculous game I played. I was beaten for one infraction or another throughout the day, anyway.

One Saturday morning he told me to go spend the day with Rory at my mom's house, so I did. When I returned, he said, "Hey bitch, guess what? You're on TV now. Don't forget to smile." Trent had cameras and recording devices installed in the apartment so that he could watch my every move: how long I was on the phone, how I treated Rory, whether I took a nap, who came to the door, how hard I worked around the apartment. When he came home at night, he would walk to the phone, hit Star 69 to see whom I had been talking to, and then would go to the closet and pull the cassettes from the recording device. He'd spend the next half-an-hour going over the tapes, making sure I was doing my job and that I didn't have sex with anybody. I was living with a man whose mind was eroding right before my eyes.

A trip to our neighborhood grocery store was particularly troublesome. Because he would take me late at night, the checkers usually seemed to always be male. It also seemed clear that the store's obvious policy was for its employees to be overly gracious. It was a flammable combination.

"That was chatty," he said as we walked to the car. "What were you talking about?"

"He asked how I was. I told him I was doing fine. That was it."

"It seemed like it was more than that."

"No."

"I don't know, Jessica—there was more talking than that."

"He asked me if I found everything okay. I told him I did."

"So you did say more than just 'fine.'"

"Yeah, but that was it."

He grabbed my arm. "Well let's just be clear. You lied when you said that was all you said because that wasn't all you said, bitch. That wasn't all you said. That's how you get yourself in trouble. It's fucking dumb to lie. Do you understand me?"

"I understand."

"Now what was that little part at the end?"

"He asked if I needed help to my car."

"Did you want him to walk you to the car?"

"No."

"Are you sure?"

"Yes."

"Bitch is lying to me."

"I'm not lying."

"I can see it in your eyes. Bitch is lying to me. Goddamn you, motherfucker. You wanted that dude to walk you to your car!"

Trent's extreme insecurities closed in on him in a moment's notice, turning a hello, fine, thank you or goodbye into a come-on and betrayal. He was a strong man, but his infrastructure was built with twigs. He beat me and sodomized me that night.

After I returned home following my three days at Helen's, his madness burst forth like a crystal pitcher of water set down on a burning stove. He actually found a way to ratchet up all forms of brutality, turning my entire body into a horrific, unsightly sore.

Many nights I would lie next to him in bed and think that all I needed was a steady hand clasped around a pistol and I could put an end to it all. I could hide it in my underwear and he would never see it beneath my nightgown as I came out of the shower. I could just lie down next to him and place it against his temple as he slept. Bang. It'd all be over.

But if I somehow managed to screw it up, he would turn on me so viciously I would be dead before I knew what hit me. Maybe that was really the answer. I could try to take him out, and if I died in the process, it would be worth it. He would be dead or I would be dead. Anything would be better than this. I did think about taking my own life. I wondered if I could do it. If I didn't have Rory, I surely would have. I was ready to die.

On the way home from work one evening, he stopped by his favorite bar and managed to get into a fight. He ended up coming home with a broken foot. To have him somewhat immobilized and on the couch was a welcome reprieve from never knowing whether I was about to be attacked.

Still, I was at the end of my rope. There were times I would simply look at Rory and begin crying. I would pick him up and sing and hold him as we danced in our living room long enough for my tears to go away and I could smile and laugh and show him that everything was okay. I was the crying mother who was dancing to save her life and living to see her son smile. One way or another, however, it seemed like Rory's life was over. If I botched it up and died trying to protect myself, Rory would have to endure a life with him. If I were to kill Trent, he would lose us both if I were to go to prison. And if we just went on as we were, he would live the nightmare of watching his father beat his mother to a pulp. What kind of person could he grow up to be? How long could I dance away the horror?

It was Saturday morning and time to do the wash. I had separated the colors and filled the basket; I sat in the kitchen and waited until he got out of bed so he could monitor my walk to the laundry room.

"I have to do laundry," I said to him as he emerged from the bedroom on his crutches.

He motioned to the door. I picked up my basket and walked out.

As I turned the corner and began to walk the sidewalk that led to the laundry room, I could see our window in my peripheral vision, but none of the blinds had been bent down to make room for him to watch me. Had he forgotten to look? Was he busy doing something else? Did he not want to hobble over on his bum foot? I began to pick up my pace to see if I could get all the way to the laundry room without being watched. Perhaps his need for constant surveillance was loosening. Suddenly, from the window now behind me and to the left, came a *snap*. It was the sound of the blind. This time was different, however. The sound cut through my body and stopped me cold. I stood there in view of the eye. I looked straight ahead. My body quivered. I thought about Rory. I thought about Trent's broken foot. I thought about my life.

I dropped my basket and ran.

15

CHEAP CLOSET DOOR

EVERY STEP TOOK ME further away from Rory, my beautiful little boy whom I had come to love more than my own life. He was my center, my geographic core, and as I dashed away, I could feel myself straining against his gravitational pull. Each step was a necessity because it took me further from Trent—but each induced its own awful pain. I was running away from my baby.

I was so horrified, I don't recall seeing anything as I ran. I had many options from which to choose a destination: four rows of apartments with two stories each, a park to the left, scrub-covered hills to the right, and the street on the far side of the complex. Somehow, without ever cognitively deciding to, I arrived at the door of the apartment manager, and I burst in.

"I'm Jessica Yaffa! I need to hide in here. Please, please keep this door locked!" I said in a panic to the manager's wife, Marni.

Marni, a gray-haired woman sitting behind her desk, drew back in her chair with shock all over her face.

"I'm so sorry!" I yelled out as I began to run down the apartment's short hallway, passing a bathroom and a bedroom, and then into a room that looked as if it was being used only to store boxes. I opened the shallow closet, stepped inside and shut the door.

Marni followed me into the room and pulled open the closet door. "What is going on here?"

"I'm in building A—do you remember me?"

"Of course. What is going on?"

"Is the door locked?"

"Yes—it's locked!"

"I'm being kept hostage in my apartment by my husband. I've run away, and I'm sure he's coming after me. I've got to get my son out of our apartment—please, call the police and don't open your door until you know it's them—will you do that for me?" I said, spitting out all the words as quickly as I could.

Suddenly we heard a violent jiggling and pounding on the front door. "I know she's fucking in there! Let me in, you fucking bitch! Jessica! Jessica!"

"That's him. Please don't let him in!" I pleaded, trying to keep my voice at a whisper.

Marni shut the closet and the bedroom door, and she went to the front door. "Who's there?" she called.

"Listen, I know Jessica is in there, so you better let me in or I'll break down this fucking door!" Trent hollered.

"Leave me alone, do you hear me? There's no Jessica here."

"Don't give me that shit, you fuck!"

"Listen, sir, I'm going to call the police."

Trent began to pound relentlessly. It sounded as if he were throwing his whole body against the door. I thought the building would cave in.

"Stop it. Stop it right now!" Marni screamed.

I heard muffled talk from Marni as she spoke on the phone; all the while Trent attacked the door, yanking at the lock. It sounded as if it might give way—as if the wood in the door jamb was beginning to rip apart.

"Fine!" she said, obviously terrified by the noise. "See for yourself!" Marni let Trent in! My eyes widened as I gasped in disbelief. The front door swung open and slammed against the wall. "You see, I told you nobody was…"

I could hear Trent as he started overturning the two front desks while Marni screamed, "Stop it, stop it!" He then thrashed about in the bathroom, and then went to the first bedroom down the hall. He upended the entire room, emptying the closet, pulling out all the clothes and pushing over the bed while Marni picked up the phone and began calling the police again. I closed my eyes and began to pray, *Please, please, please.*

He came down the hall and smashed open the door of the room I was in. In a moment, everything was still. I stood holding my breath—just a cheap closet door between me and Trent who, I was sure, would beat me lifeless. It remained quiet. He was listening for me. I opened my mouth widely and tried to exhale as slowly and quietly as my heaving lungs would allow. He made no noise. Had he left?

Suddenly, with an awful crash, he began hitting the boxes out of the way, knocking them in every direction. He then overturned the small bed. I felt a slight squeal of fear push its way out of my throat. I was holding back two terrors, each as awful as the other: the possibility that I would be found and the possibility that my baby was in danger as he was left alone in the apartment.

Trent thrashed his way across the room, and then, in an instant, he stopped. How could he not know I was there? He stood perfectly still at the closet, facing away from me. I could see a glimpse of the back of his head through the slats of the door. He was just inches from my face. He didn't move. I didn't move. Tears streamed down my cheeks.

My heart was pounding so fiercely I was afraid Trent would be able to hear it. I kept my mouth open and tried to inhale and exhale the smallest puffs of air possible, slowly, slowly. Drool flowed from my mouth. My nose ran freely. Sweat covered my face. Suddenly—and I do not know why—he bolted out of the room and then out of the apartment. I heard the door slam and lock. Marni came running to open the closet. "Honey!" she cried. "He's gone!"

I crumbled to the floor and began to sob. Marni took hold of me, "Police are coming. Don't worry. Everything is going to be okay." I stayed in that position for a few minutes until I could hear sirens in the distance. "I'm sorry, I'm so sorry," Marni said, her arms still around me.

When the noise of the sirens grew closer and I could hear the squeal of the tires of the police car, I stood up and ran to the door.

"Where are you going?" Marni yelled.

I opened the door and exited the apartment, waving my arms. "Help, help!" I screamed hysterically as the cops screeched to a halt. "You have to get my son out of my apartment! I'll tell you everything, but you just have to get my son! Please, please, please!"

The cops exited the car. "Ma'am, what's going on here?"

"I've been held hostage in my apartment by my husband—he's been beating me, and now he has my son!"

I told them that I wanted them to escort me to my apartment so I could take Rory and some clothes and leave. They said they would. Marni gave me a handful of tissues, and I wiped my face and blew my nose as we briskly walked.

When we arrived at my apartment, I was a trembling mess. One of the officers pushed open the door. "Mr. Michaels," he said. As we got up the half level of stairs to the landing, Trent was sitting on the floor with Rory, calmly watching TV. "Sir, we are here with your wife, and she's going to take the baby and some clothes and she's going to leave and you're not going to get up or say a word, is that understood?"

Trent said nothing.

The officer picked up Rory, who was busy watching cartoons, and handed him to me. I cried even harder once he was in my arms. "Mommy's so sorry, sweetie. Mommy's so sorry."

I hurried into my room, grabbed a bag, threw some clothes inside, along with a few of Rory's clothes and began to walk out of the house when I noticed an envelope lying by the phone. I took it and walked outside with the police.

"I want to press charges," I said. "He's been beating me."

"Has he hit you today?" the officer said.

"Not today, but—"

"Has he hit your son?"

"No."

"Then we don't have battery. This is a domestic disturbance."

I answered their questions so they could make their report and pleaded with them to hurry up so I could get the hell out of there. They walked me to my car and explained how to get a restraining order.

With Rory in the back in his car seat and my bag of clothes in the passenger seat, I began to drive away. I pulled the envelope out of the bag and lay it on top. *Lyndi Sullivan, 4588 Tulip, Los Angeles.*

I got on the 5 Freeway and headed north. I knew the cops were still with Trent and he would have no idea of where I was going. Even so, I floored it.

∞∞∞∞

It was so great to know there was no way in the world he was going to find me.

Yes indeed. Safe for now. What a relief!

Hmm.

What.

Well I'm just curious to know, why do you say *for now?* Why don't you think that's the end of my story? I mean, after all I've been through, why do you assume there's more?

Well, with a guy like Trent, there's always more, in one way or another.

Hmm.

So is there more, Jessica?

You wouldn't believe.

16

SPLINTERED WOOD

Dear Jessica

Sometimes it occurs to me that years have gone by that we have had no communication and when I sit and really think about it, everything about it feels so wrong! I miss you, my dear, sweet friend. Besides your lovely way, I miss our talks about men and how your voice and advice has meant so much to me. In fact, I could use a little good advice right now! Let's get in touch soon!

I love you,

Lyndi

P.S. Are you still with Trent?

Lyndi Sullivan was about the sweetest girl I had ever known. The day—no, the minute we met on the playground in kindergarten I knew she was going to be my best friend. She was cute and funny and smiley and warm. What was not to love? Funny thing is, even

though I walked home that day with the name Lyndi Sullivan dancing around my head, the next time I saw her—in fact, every time I
saw her for the next couple weeks—she couldn't remember my name.
No matter. I had patience. She was going to be my best friend ever.

And she was.

Even though by the sixth grade, 90 miles separated us—with her
living in Los Angeles and me now in San Diego—we still wrote and
called on birthdays and special occasions and even got to see each
other during the summers from time to time. We had become the
kind of friends that were bonded spiritually and knew we would be
for the rest of our lives.

As we grew older, boys became the main topic of discussion,
and we talked each other through the rigors of trying to be attractive
and what kind of personality traits got the best response and all the
highs and lows of our brief encounters with them in class or in the
hallways. She was my lifeline.

There were times when we were very consistent in our communication but sometimes, when life got in the way, it got spotty.
On a few occasions, a year would pass. Her card had been sitting
next to my bed for two weeks and was something I was going to
answer as soon as I had a moment. Life with Trent did not lend
itself to letter-writing or long phone calls. But I also knew that no
matter how much time had passed, we would always be best friends.
And if there were anybody in this world who would take me in, it
would be Lyndi.

I pulled off the freeway to find a Thomas Guide map of Los
Angeles. I found one at a gas station, located the page that showed
4588 Tulip and ripped it from the guide. I charged some gas and a
small carton of milk, sat in the parking lot, gave Rory a quick change
and some food from his diaper bag. All I had were Cheerios and some
string cheese.

"We really did it," I said to him, trying to hide the fact that I was
shaking on the inside. He had just woken from a nap and seemed to

be in good spirits. I hugged and kissed him. We had just changed our lives.

We made it to Lyndi's in about 45 minutes. She was in her driveway washing her car when we pulled up. She looked at me as if she didn't recognize me. I'm not sure if it was because I had surprised her or I was now somebody else.

When she realized who I was, she dropped her hose and hurried toward me with a delighted squeal. I ran toward her like she was the key to our survival—I almost ran right through her, and once I had her, I didn't want to let go. We sat on her porch, Rory in her arms, and before I could tell her why I was there, I let out a terrible cry. I was gasping for air. I must have scared her to death.

When I finally managed to explain everything, she was only too happy to let us stay with her. "As long as you want," she said over and over. Her face was filled with concern, and she even cried over the lonely and painful road that her dear friend had traveled. Still there was a moment when I detected a look that said, *Well I'm not surprised.* She always was highly suspicious of Trent.

Over the next week, I hired a lawyer and filed for a restraining order. I learned that Trent had to be allowed to see Rory; were I to keep Rory from him, I would be held in contempt of court. I figured as soon as I called my mom, I would learn how much Trent had been bugging her about seeing Rory, just like last time. I put it off as long as I could. I also started calling on apartments from ads I saw in the *Union Tribune,* a San Diego paper Lyndi bought me from a newsstand. She encouraged me to take it easy for a day or two and relax, to try to heal, think, cry and look long into Rory's eyes and reassure him that everything was okay. I tried it for about an hour. It was awful. I couldn't sit still. It was as if I had guzzled a dozen cups of coffee and my mind was spinning in loud, roaring overdrive. I knew that if the spinning ever stopped, however, I'd actually have to think and feel—I wasn't certain my heart could take it. The spinning was my protection.

With graduation fast approaching and a job as a counselor to severely emotionally disturbed children waiting for me once I had my degree, I knew I had to go back home to San Diego. I called my mom, told her my ordeal and asked for her to help me out with finances. She didn't flinch. "Of course," she said. Lyndi bought me more diapers and food than I could handle plus a basket of goodies and a sleeping bag and some blankets. "Listen to me," she said as she stood outside my car window on the day Rory and I were leaving. She held my hand as the engine idled. "You've been dealing with unthinkable oppression for the last six years. Any other woman might have fallen to pieces. But you, in addition to dealing with an asshole like Trent, taking care of a home, you are raising a son, finishing college with honors, getting job offers, and you're still not even 23 years old. I've spent my life being impressed by you but I have never been more in awe of you than I am now. He tried to take away your sweetness, he tried to break you, he tried to pry you from your son, but he couldn't do it. Jessica, you are strong. You will make it."

Moved and in tears, I swung the car door open and stepped out to hug her one more time before going back into my life. Rory and I got on the freeway, heading toward the apartment I had my eye on, in a neighborhood a half hour from where Trent and I had been living.

Two hours later, we were at the apartment, meeting with the manager, agreeing to the terms and giving him a deposit. We walked into our tiny, empty apartment; I dropped my stuff, went to a pay phone, called the cops, and told them my plans. Then I called my mom and told her I was fine and that I wouldn't be telling her where I now lived for a while. She accepted it. She knew the drill.

About an hour later, two officers met me at Trent's and my old apartment to escort me inside so I could get my belongings. When we arrived, we opened the door to find that Trent was not there. In fact, it appeared that he hadn't been there for a while and that he wasn't coming back. The furniture and appliances were still there, but everything that was his—clothes, toiletries and CDs—were gone.

On my way back to my new apartment, I stopped at a hardware store and bought a cheap, portable home alarm and went home to install it as well as rig my windows to never be opened without me knowing it. I stopped by to meet my neighbors on both sides, telling them as little as I could about my situation, but asking them to call the police if they ever saw my signal to them—my lights quickly switching on and off repeatedly. They saw that I was a young, single woman with a two-and-a-half-year-old son and probably put two and two together—plus the fact that I was all business. They were very kind, even though on my first day I was already bringing the possibility of danger into their quiet lives.

That night, I snuggled up with Rory on the floor under some blankets and on top of a sleeping bag. I found myself looking out the window at the stars as I stroked his curly hair. As calm as the moment seemed, two sides of my mind seemed to be in a battle for what I would think about. Memories of the many horrors I had just endured over the last six years would seep in, and then almost as quickly, other thoughts would storm in and push them away, saying, *Not now. There'll be plenty of time to think about that later.* I prayed for protection and a normal, happy life for Rory.

Rory fell right to sleep, and soon, I did too, but every now and then I would raise my hand to touch under the edge of the sleeping bag, just beneath a magazine, where I kept a knife.

Trent must have asked around the office. He learned a restraining order meant that he still had rights to see his child—and it wasn't long before he let my mom know this is exactly what he intended to do.

I asked my mom to pass along that I would call him at his work at a time of my choosing, and that he should answer his phone, because if he missed my call, it would only delay seeing Rory. On a Friday morning, I gathered up my courage and nervously walked over to a pay phone. It was 8:01 a.m., one minute past Trent's starting time at work.

"Hello?"

"Trent, it's Jessica," I said trying to be short to show him I wasn't interested in conversation. "I'm going to be at my mom's house on Tuesday at 5:30. You can come and see Rory then. You'll have one hour to play with him and then I'm going to leave with Rory. After I do, you must stay in your car at my mom's for 20 minutes before you can get back on the road. If you leave before then, my mom will be forced to call the cops, okay? This will be an opportunity for you to play with Rory, but it will not be a time to try to talk to me. If you don't come on Tuesday, you will have to wait to set up another time."

"What is this?" he protested. "That's not how this is supposed to go."

"Well this is how I have to do it. Last thing, I have a great relationship with the police, and they know about our meeting time and will be on alert. That's it for now. See you Tuesday."

I put the phone down and nearly collapsed. *I hope he bought the part about the police,* I thought to myself.

When Tuesday came, I was waiting by the window, watching for Trent. He pulled up at 5:30 on the nose. I walked outside and stood on the porch of my mom's house with Rory in my arms. "Stay strong, stay strong," I whispered to myself.

"Hi," he said as he got out of the car and came around the front. I didn't say anything. As he approached, I held Rory close. "Daddy's going to play with you for a little while and you're going to have a lot of fun. I'm going to be inside with grandma, okay, sweetie?" I lathered him up with kisses and put him down on the ground, still holding his hand.

"Hi, Rory. Daddy's so happy to see you!" Trent said as he came close. He knelt down and picked Rory up. I let go of Rory's hand and began to walk back into the house. "I'm going to change my ways, Jessica. You're going to see a completely different person," he said.

I paid him no mind and closed the door. I went back over to the window and sat down to watch. He saw me. That's how I wanted it.

I hoped he thought I looked tough. Had he been able to look close enough, he would have seen that I was shaking violently.

Trent started playing with Rory, and there were moments when he got something out of him, but mostly it was stiff and awkward. Rory, who had been thrown into the middle of this completely inauthentic try at having a relationship, looked confused or disinterested. Trent was trying to achieve the impossible: jump into a kid's life and make him have fun whether he was up to it or not. It was a loser from the start.

A difficult-to-watch hour passed. I walked out of the house. "It's been an hour, Trent," I said. "Alright, Rory, say goodbye to daddy." Trent actually looked relieved. I can't say I blamed him. It looked like hard work. He kissed Rory and told him how much fun he had and turned him back over to me without much hesitation.

"Our house is going to be full of love, Jessica, you will see," he said.

"Nope, nope, nope," I said curtly, turning around to go back into the house. I paused before entering. "We'll make this a standing thing. Every Tuesday and Friday at 5:30. Stay in your car for 20 minutes after I leave." I shut the door. My mom took the position at the window, I grabbed Rory and my things, walked out the side of the house to my car, backed out of her driveway and left, watching my rearview mirror like a hawk.

My mom reported to me that Trent had stayed in his car. He didn't read. He didn't look around. He just stared straight ahead, glancing down to his watch from time to time. When 20 minutes were up, he left. It had been a success, even though my body was reacting like it was having a near-death experience, and my emotions were shot. Still, it had worked.

The following Tuesdays were much the same. Trent would pick up Rory and use our brief moments together to kindly tell me how much life was going to be better for us while I would simply raise a *don't-talk-to-me* hand. I was trying to take the high road, but little by little, there was a growing tension inside my heart. I had a strong desire to get some things off my chest, and my plan to stay silent as he did all the talking was wearing thin on my unjustly beaten-down bones. I began to hate the imbalance I felt as he got to slip in a few choice words while all I would do was turn my back and walk away. I began to entertain his comments a bit more so I could have the satisfaction of putting a blunt end to his plans for a future together.

Before long, it was clear that Tuesdays had very little to do with Rory. We spent most of the time that he was supposed to be playing, arguing—him making the case that we could restore our relationship and me making the case that that was a joke. He found in his demented mind the ability to blame me for breaking up our family. "I'm not the one who ran away. I'm not the one who can't be trusted. I'm not the one who takes marriage lightly," he'd say. It was disgusting.

"You can't seem to get it that we aren't getting back together, can you?" I'd say. "This is not a temporary arrangement. This is forever. Get on with your life."

His aggression grew—I could hear it in his voice and see it in his body language. One day, when he finally seemed to understand that I was never coming home with him, he got so mad that I thought he was going to rip off his car door. We were absolutely on the wrong course. I had to set new boundaries.

It was just a bit before 5:30 on a Friday and we were at my mom's house waiting for Trent. The phone rang. My mom answered it; it was my aunt, Nora. I asked her to call Aunt Nora back because I was uncomfortable with my mom being distracted when Trent showed up, which would be at any moment. She held her finger up to say she just wanted a minute and would get off the phone. I couldn't blame her. I knew why she wanted the time with her sister, whom she loved dearly. Between the collapse of my marriage, concern for Rory's well-being, the loss of her husband, Sam's devastation and my severe financial woes, the loving voice of Aunt Nora was probably just what her heart needed.

"So how is Ronnie?" my mom asked spryly. "You're kidding. Well, that's great to hear. How long was he there?" She stood up and began to walk.

I looked at mom as if to say, *Don't get into anything too long, now.* She tends to like to walk around while on the phone, and she started to pace back and forth from the kitchen to the dining room. From what I could tell, everything about her—from what she was doing to how she sounded—had the makings of a much longer conversation than a mere minute.

"Well, awful," she said to Aunt Nora. "She is living the nightmare of having to deal with Trent, and I just don't know how she does it..."

Trent, who had parked and was walking across the grass toward the front door, heard my mom talking. He burst into the house like a truck ramming the front door. My mom who was at the sink, looked up in shock to see Trent enter her kitchen. "Get my fucking business out of your mouth, do you hear me, you fucking bitch?"

I was holding and playing with Rory in my old bedroom. I ran out of the room and down the hall to find Trent standing in the kitchen yelling at my mom with her cowering beside him. "Trent! What are you doing?" I yelled.

"Next time I hear my business coming out of her mouth, hell's going to come down on this house. Do you understand me?" he bit back.

"Get out of this house and leave!" I demanded.

"Bitch thinks that now that she's all out on her own that she can talk any way she wants to me."

"You're out of control and I don't have to listen to this. Now get out of here!"

I rushed back down the hall to my room, shut the door and locked it. I heard, "Fuck you, mother fucker!"

He ran to my room, and my mom followed after, screaming at him as he pounded on my door. "Trent, get out of here right now!" my mom shrieked.

"I'm going to beat your ass, and I'm going to beat your mom's ass. I'm not afraid of either of you, do you understand me? I'll fucking lay waste to you both. Now give me back my boy!"

The house was an echo chamber of screams. I was screaming at him from inside my room. Rory was screaming as he cried. My mom was screaming at him from the other side of the door. Trent was screaming at me as he was hitting the door so hard I thought it was going to break. It was pandemonium. Trent drew back and began to kick at the door. The house began to shake. Boom. Boom. Boom. Each of us began to shriek even louder. Suddenly the door broke from the hinges and the entire thing fell in, splintered wood and all. He charged into the room, and I stood there shocked and unable to make a sound. He walked directly to me. "No, Trent" I quivered. "Please." He grabbed Rory from my arms with an awful force. To try to hold on to Rory would be to pull him apart. I had to let go. I immediately broke into tears.

He slapped me, grabbed me by my neck and threw me onto the bed. With Rory still in his arms, he straddled me and put his hands around my neck, just like he always did, and squeezed hard enough for me to get the point: no matter what I may have started to think these last weeks, *he* had the power. "*My* son. Don't ever think you can take my son from me," he said. He spit in my face. He pushed my neck with full force and got off me. He walked out, passing my mom, who was kneeling in the hall in shock and nearly unable to breathe.

I got off the bed, chased after him and began pleading. "Please don't drive away, Trent! Please! You're in no condition to be driving with Rory!"

"Shut the fuck up," he said as he walked out of the house. He tossed Rory in the front seat of his car and screeched away.

17

EXCHANGE GONE WRONG

"MY HUSBAND HAS MY little boy and we just had a fight and he's furious and his car doesn't have a car seat and he has just choked me and kicked the door down in my mom's house and my son is in danger!" I frantically screamed to the 911 operator.

Ten minutes later when the cops arrived, they took a report, snapped photos of the door laying in the room and the bruising around my neck. They also cared for my traumatized mother, whose face was white with anguish and bereft of any energy. She had gone from excited to talk to Aunt Nora to devastated and in shock in just a few seconds. It was more than her body could take. Her eyes told the story. *I've had it*, they said.

Police units had been dispatched into the community to look for Trent's car and the officers who were with me were asking for information about where I thought he might go. I didn't have a lot to offer. I couldn't think of anywhere he would take Rory except for his apartment, but I didn't even know where that was. Just before they left, I had a spark of an idea.

"I heard Trent on the phone with a female coworker several times," I told them. "They were always a little chummier than I thought they should be. I always thought they had something going on. Oh, and I think she's Spanish."

"Got the number to the office?" the officer asked.

The police discovered the only female who worked with Trent was a woman named Maria Quinones. They promptly went to her apartment. Maria was there with Rory, who was plopped in front of the TV. Trent was nowhere to be found.

An hour and a half after, the police pulled up again to my mom's house. I burst open the door and ran outside sobbing. A woman from Child Protective Services handed him to me, and I hugged and smothered him with kisses and told him how sorry I was, over and over again. "I want to press charges," I told the officer.

The officer closed his notebook. "We'll turn in our report, but my guess is that the D.A. isn't going to pursue this."

"Are you kidding? Why not?" I said, motioning to my bruised neck. I was infuriated.

He wanted no part of where I was about to take this conversation and spoke sternly. "Look, I'm not here to make her case, ma'am, but my guess is that she'll see this as an exchange gone wrong and nothing more. But let's just wait and see. If your mom wants to pursue a charge for the door, that's another matter."

I was overjoyed to have Rory back in my arms, but I was beginning to see the police as almost no defense against a dangerous thug whose only target was me. It appeared I had nowhere to turn. When they left, I came close to my still-trembling mom as she sat on the bed. "Jess," she said. "I can't do this, honey. You'll have to find somewhere else to exchange Rory. I'm sorry, but I can't go through this anymore. I'm scared for you and Rory. I'm scared for Sam. And I'm scared for me."

"I understand," I replied, my arm around her shoulders. "I do, I really do." In my mind, I was thinking, *What in the world am I going to do now?*

Mom stood, took my hand and dropped it on my lap, walked to her bedroom, shut the door and then locked it. I sat there crushed under the weight of the guilt. I had only two people in my life and I was bringing both of them so much pain. My poor mom and dad had talked to me relentlessly about breaking up with Trent and now this was the result of my rebellion. My son sits inside dirty apartments with a woman he doesn't know, is the object of a police rescue, and takes rides in cop cars, sirens blaring, with guns nearby. My mom now sits shaking in her room wondering what her life has come to. All of it was because of me.

I looked back over my life and realized how much lying I had done to get here. I lied my way through college and then covered up the truth about what was really going on with me and Trent to keep her from knowing that I made an awful mistake by not listening to her. My beautiful mother had been there for me every time I asked and even knew to step closer when she suspected I needed her most. She had always deserved the truth, but I couldn't give it to her. Not even now, especially not now. It would destroy what was left of her.

I stood up from the bed and walked to the kitchen, all the while shaking my head in disbelief.

I readied Rory, packed up our stuff and looked at the clock. It was now nearly 9 p.m. I needed to get on the road. There was no telling if Trent was perched somewhere watching the front of the house so he could follow me home, but what could I do about that now? Just then, the phone rang.

"Hello?" I answered.

"I still want to see my son."

∞∞∞

I had felt alone before, but I think this was different.

> Are you talking about your mom's reaction?

Yeah. That really hit hard. I know she didn't love me less. I know she was just doing what she had to do to protect herself, but between being on my own in a secret apartment, seemingly no cops to turn to and being on the run from Trent, her telling me that I was now a threat to her safety, Sam's safety, Rory's safety—even my own, well, that hurt. She was absolutely right, but it still hurt. I think I felt more alone then than at any other time.

> Why do you think you felt more alone than when you were actually more alone?

You mean before I had Rory?

> Yes.

I don't know. I think there's something about Rory's eyes that sort of made it that way.

> That's interesting. Can you explain?

I may have been more alone at other times, but when he looked at me, he was looking *to* me, in a sense, you know what I mean? I guess he was saying, in a way, you're going to get me through this, right? And honestly, I didn't know how I was going to do it. I didn't feel there was anybody on my side. It was me, just me that had to make his fears go away. And so far I had done nothing but fail. Does that make sense?

> Yes, I think it does.

And that made me feel more alone. I mean, with my mom disallowing us from making exchanges at her house, I just felt like there wasn't much padding between me and the total collapse of my life.

> You certainly were taking it from all sides.

That is how it felt. Did I tell you about Maria, the girl from Trent's work?

The one Trent left Rory with?
Yes.

What about her?
She had an infant with her when the cops arrived. It was Trent's.

18

PARK AND PUKE

I TRIED TO KEEP MY BREATHING SHORT as I drove. I was afraid that if I let my lungs fill too much, a large exhale would ignite my gag reflex, and I would vomit all over the car as I had done before. My body trembled so violently and my face wore my terror so broadly that it would trigger panic in Rory. He knew exactly what it all meant even though I never said anything about where we were going. I just couldn't get myself to tell him I was taking him to his daddy, who would then take him away from me.

"I don't want to see daddy, mommy," he'd say as he wept bitterly. "Rory scared, mommy."

Tears would flow down my face to hear his little voice plead with his mommy who he thought was his protector.

Trent had learned that even though I had a restraining order against him, his rights as a father were still intact—not only was he allowed to see his son, he could take him away from me, and there

143

was nothing I could do about it. After everything he had done to me, as well as all that he had just done to Rory, plus the entire episode at my mother's house, I still had to deliver Rory to him personally if I couldn't find anybody else to do it. Then I had to watch him drive away with my baby who was scared to death of him. Trent didn't even have to tell me where he was taking him and often wouldn't. Restraining order? What a joke.

The terror of it all would make my body wrench so violently I would often throw up on the way to make the exchange, definitely after the exchange and would remain completely sick to my stomach and overcome with grief the entire time he was gone, sometimes as many as three hours.

Our new location for exchanging Rory was the police station. An officer explained that all police stations could serve as neutral, safe ground for exchanges, which ultimately proved to be true, if by safe one means safe from physical attack. But the station was no defense against verbal assault. Trent used the time to hurl obscenities at me as if the exchanges were meant especially for that. He was vicious, emerging from his car in mid rant. "Fucking bitch thinks she can traipse all around town, giving pussy to every fucker she meets. Ain't that right, bitch? You have a son at home and you're acting like that? Give me my boy and get the fuck out of here. And why don't you go home and think about how you broke a family up and how your actions are killing your son."

I would pull Rory from the car and walk his innocent body toward Trent like I was walking him toward a raging fire—everything in me wanted to run the other way. "Please just take him and go."

Every word I said set him off. "No mother fucker going to tell me what to do with my son. You mind your own fucking business, which to you means being anywhere but in your home with your family. Let me ask you something. Why you looking for everything that you got at home with me? I got ten inches right here."

"I'm out of here, Trent. Please be careful with Rory, please, I'm begging you," I'd say.

I would give Rory a last kiss while he screamed and reached for me. Pulling away in my car, I could hear Rory's cries and a final "Fuck you!" from Trent. I would pull into a quiet neighborhood as my body heaved and pitched forward. I would slam on the brakes and reach for my bag that I kept on the passenger seat, violently throwing up the remaining contents of my stomach. And yet as bad as it was, it was about to get worse.

Rory's limited vocabulary began to grow in ways that were terrifying. "Fuck! Dick! Sex!" Rory would say. "Fuck. Dick! Sex!"

I would ask where he was hearing such words, trying to keep my voice calm, so as not to betray their emotional power. "Me and daddy watch pow-pow movies."

"Pow-pow movies? Other kinds of movies, too?"

It was clear my two-and-a-half year old was in an emotional grinder, being moved back and forth between two parents, witnessing one verbally assault the other and watching violent movies and pornography.

I had hoped that over the months, Rory would warm up to the idea of spending time with Trent, but it never happened. He cried profusely every time we drove to make the exchange, as if I were asking him to step into his nightmare over and over. One day, as he cried inconsolably in the backseat, he said, "Daddy hits." I never saw any evidence on Rory's body to suggest that he had been hit by Trent, and of course, as someone who had been hit for a long time, I knew the kind of damage even a minor swat could produce. I realized that Rory's frightened words could have meant that he had seen Trent hit me, and perhaps that is what scared him so much. No matter, hearing Rory talk of hitting immediately brought back the horrors of my life under the fist of Trent, and it sent my body into overdrive. I began to panic uncontrollably. I pulled over, tried to get out an apology to Rory and then vomited as my emotions twisted my body like a wet towel. When we arrived at the police station, this time it was me who emerged from the car in mid rant. "I do not know what goes on when you have Rory, but I want to make it very clear that you may not strike my baby even in the smallest way, do you understand me, Trent? Hitting of any kind is absolutely not allowed!"

"Get the fuck out of here before I pound you into the ground," he said. "And don't even think you can tell me how to raise my child. You want to see someone get hit, bitch? You want to see that?"

It was an awful exchange. By the way Rory sat terrified in his car seat, I could tell he felt every word of the violence we spoke to each other. The daggers that Trent and I were throwing at each other were slicing through him. I looked in his sad eyes. We were ripping our son's soul apart.

Officer Hickam, who watched many of the exchanges from afar, walked up to me after Trent drove away. "Ms. Yaffa, I'm getting a little tired watching you make exchanges. Don't you think coming here is an overreaction? I mean he hasn't laid a hand on you."

I gave him a *you stupid idiot* look and got inside my car and drove on over to my favorite quiet neighborhood to park and puke.

Three months worth of twice-a-week exchanges left me physically weak and emotionally spent as I regularly exploded into horrible bouts of weeping and vomiting. *This can't go on*, I would think to myself, now 15 pounds lighter than when it all began. *There has to be an end to this, there just has to be. Think, Jessica, think. You must figure out a way to make this stop.* Mercifully, one day, it would.

It was a Thursday around 2 p.m. Rory was in the backseat, in tears, trying to tell me that he was scared and didn't want to see his daddy. I was coaching myself through each mile. *Stay calm, Jessica, just one more mile.* When I arrived at the station, Trent was waiting and popped out of his car. He started in as he usually did—only today there was something new to set him off.

"Where did you get this car, bitch?"

I had taken out a loan with the help of my mother. I was able to get a new used car to replace my trashy little Ford that was nearly 16 years old. My new car was a shiny Nissan Sentra and it probably looked more expensive than it was. I had had it only a day, and it had been polished and detailed just before I bought it.

"Answer me, bitch. Where did you get this?"

I got out of the car. "Are you going to have him for two hours or three today, Trent?"

"You don't have the money for a car like this! Where are you getting this kind of money?"

"Two or three hours? How many today, Trent?"

"You must be fucking somebody to be driving a car like this. Who's the asshole who bought you this car?"

"Trent, knock it off," I said.

"You're fucking another man! You're fucking another man! Don't you see what this is doing to me?"

"Stop it right now!"

"Bitch, you can't scrape together two pennies. There is only one way to drive a car like this. You have a motherfucking boyfriend!" He waved his hands and stormed around. He had come unglued.

"You're out of control and I don't have to listen to this. I'm not going to get into where I got it because it's none of your business." I sat back in the car, closed the door and locked it. Trent bent down and put his face up to the window. "What do you think you're doing?"

"Like I'm going to let you take Rory while you're in this condition," I said through the window.

"So you're just going to take him? Just like that? You think you can just take him away from me?"

"Look," I said, "until you can show me that you've calmed down, he's not getting out of this car."

"Bitch, you open this car door, or I will tear it off," he screamed. He put his hand on my door handle and started to yank.

I looked around for cops. There weren't any. "Trent, I'm just going to drive around for an hour and then I'll come back here to meet you after you've had some time to cool down."

"You're not going anywhere! Now get out the car!" He gave a heavy rap to the top of my car with his fist. *Womp.*

"Stop that, Trent!" I turned the ignition and began to back out of the parking space.

"Don't make me do this, Jessica. You don't want this!"

"Just give me one hour then I'll come back—please!" I pleaded. I pulled forward and headed for the street. I watched him stand there in my rearview mirror. I turned onto the street. As I did, I saw Trent dash toward his car.

"Oh, shit!" I said.

I floored my car, thinking to myself of the insanity of driving *away* from a police station while I felt my life was in danger. I knew Trent saw me head east, so when I saw an immediate green light at the next street, I made a U-turn to see if I could throw him off. As I passed back in front of the police station, I saw Trent coming out of the parking lot, and he did exactly as I hoped. He turned east. We were going opposite directions.

But where would I go? If I tried to go back to the apartment, I couldn't be sure that somehow, I might be leading him there. I had to find somewhere else to go but couldn't think of any place safer than being back at the police station. For the moment, Rory wasn't screaming. I looked back and his eyes even looked heavy. He had put his pacifier in his mouth.

I decided to head back to the police station, but I wanted to take side streets to keep from being seen. I headed into the entrance of a newly built housing development—thinking that might give me some cover—but as I did, I heard a screech. It was Trent.

I shot into the development with Trent right behind me. I yanked my wheel hard, turned down a street, and I stepped on the gas. It was a one-way street with little room on either side. Even so, Trent slammed his gas pedal and angrily passed me. He skidded and cranked his steering wheel so that his car came to a stop facing mine head on. I slammed on the brakes. He stepped on the gas and I thought, *Shit! He's going to kill me!* With his son in my car, he rammed me at full speed. The impact jolted my head back. I immediately reached for Rory's hand; his eyes were wide with fear. He began to scream. I looked back. Trent flung open his door.

I felt tears well up in my eyes immediately. "Oh no, oh no, oh no," I said. Trent, eyes fixed on me, ran and jumped onto the top of my car holding something in his hand. He began pounding it against the windshield. "Motherfucker! I'm going to kill you, motherfucker!" he screamed at the top of his lungs.

I was shrieking so hard I thought my throat was going to come apart. Rory was hysterical. Just then I remembered that my mother had bought me a cell phone for emergencies. I dug it out of my bag. I fumbled with it and it nearly fell out of my hand. I pulled the antenna and frantically dialed 911.

"911. Can I have your location?"

"My husband is on top of my windshield and he's trying to smash it open and he's going to kill me!" I screamed.

"Your husband is breaking your windshield?" she asked.

"Yes! He's about to break through. Help me—please!"

"I gave you everything, Jessica! I gave you everything!" Trent bellowed, his fist slamming against the glass.

"Well drive away, honey!" she said, knowing that I may not know to do the obvious.

I hit the accelerator and rocked back and forth against Trent's car. "I can't!"

At that moment, Trent punched a hole and started pulling open the glass. "I'm going to kill you, bitch!" His bloody fingers were inches from my face.

"Can you go into reverse?" the operator frantically asked.

"What—I think so!"

"Well, do it now!"

I shot into reverse and Trent flew off the hood and landed in the street. I backed my rear end into a car and then forced my gas pedal to the floor as I screeched down the neighborhood street, clipping two parked cars as I fought for control. I got on the main road and turned toward in the direction of the police department. As I looked at my rearview mirror, a car shot out of the neighborhood as if by a cannon. It was Trent. He was on my tail. From my cell phone wedged between my legs, I heard the 911 operator tell me to go to the police station where officers would be waiting.

I screeched around the corner. The police station was dead ahead on the left. As I got closer I saw two cop cars in front and six or seven cops at the ready. I came barreling across the street and skidded to a stop in front of the cop cars.

"Get my baby, get my baby!" I screamed as I swung the door open and ran toward the cops. One of them, a female officer, rushed toward me. All the others crouched behind their vehicles with guns drawn. The female police officer put her arms around me as we heard tires squealing and an engine bearing down. She pulled me behind a brick wall and we covered up.

"My baby, did they get him?" I asked, trembling.

"They got him, they got him!" she said.

Trent screeched to a stop and got out. "Fuck you! Fuck you motherfucker!"

"Get down! Down on the ground!" the officers shouted. I could hear the sharp clicking of the rifles being readied.

Trent tried to run through the line of cops. "I'm going to kill you, you bitch!" he howled. They tackled Trent. Even though he had a number of knees against his body and a boot against the back of his head, like a snake with a hand around his neck, he squirmed against the strong holds of the police.

With his face being pushed into the asphalt, I could hear his contorted mouth give up the last vestiges of what was once a tender love. His soul bellowed like a beaten demon, long and awful, "Jessica! Jessica!"

19

THE SLOW CREEP
OF NORMALCY

THE DAYS FOLLOWING Trent's arrest were surreal. I was like a person who had been frozen along the side of a mountain centuries ago and suddenly thawed in modern day. Everything was new and confusing and my steps were uncertain. I had been separated from Trent before, but he had remained out there for me to fear. Now, he was behind bars. My liberation was a strange thing. I didn't know what to do with myself once every day was no longer a grimaced fight for sanity and survival.

I was 24 years old but felt 50. I was exhausted, an exhaustion that I didn't really get a sense of until everything went quiet. Sometimes I would go to my mom's house, and she would play with Rory and I would sit on the couch. No talking. No reading. The TV was off. I would just sit and stare. What just happened? What do I do now? Who am I supposed to be?

As the days passed, I started to have a strange feeling that I was being followed. Nobody was there and I knew nobody was there. But I had just had to look anyway. With time, the feeling began to startle me less and less, to the point where I rather expected it. One day I felt it again, but this time, I didn't look. I just stopped what I was doing and looked straight ahead. I knew who it was. It was my dad. It wasn't as though he had passed through celestial realms to haunt me. It was all me. The stranger following me was my creation, my doing. I was suddenly longing for my dad again. It had been four years since he had died, and all that time, my life was so filled up with Trent that I never grieved. It was at once painful and beautiful—painful because I missed him so much. But beautiful because I was doing something I should have been doing a long time ago; it felt right to become reacquainted with feelings about my dad—as if finally stepping into who I was.

In the meantime, Rory was an enigma to me. I couldn't tell what was in my little boy's heart and soul, how deep his wounds. He played and had fun with his grandma and me, but what was the truth about him? What would come to the surface and when?

My lawyer called to give me some very good news: I would not have to testify against Trent. The 911 recording of my phone call was so graphic that the judge saw it as sufficient. Trent went straight to jail from the holding tank. His sentence was eight and a half months on child endangerment, terrorist threats and assault with a deadly weapon.

The good news didn't make a dent in my mental mode, however. My brain was still in a full-court press, still trying hard to make sense of my life, like a crew of investigators tries to gather all the pieces of an airplane to determine how it blew up. Whereas before, I would sometimes sit and stare out the window, it increased to many times throughout the day. I would find myself on the couch, just running over and over the moments of my life, hoping, as I searched, to find answers as to how I got here. After a time, I did notice some changes in myself, however. A couple of times I would actually think about something, then stop thinking about it, then realize that while thinking about it, a thought about Trent never broke in to disrupt it. While that was progress, it was a bit frightening as well. I realized that if my mind was an intersection jammed with thoughts, Trent was usually directing traffic.

About four and a half months later, my mom got a call while I just happened to be over at her house.

"It's from who?" my mom said on the phone. "Trent Michaels?" She looked at me, brows furrowed. "Hold on one minute," she said to the operator.

"It's collect from Trent. What should I do?" It's amazing that months of progress could be shattered in a moment's notice. I didn't respond. "Jess," my mom said, "what should I do?"

"I don't know," I replied. "Accept it, I guess. Maybe he needs to get information from us about something."

"I'll accept," my mom said.

"Lillian, this is Trent. I need to talk to you."

My mom's face got stern. "What do you want?"

"I need to tell you how sorry I am for all that I put you and Jessica through and I see very clearly now the error of my ways. I know that Jessica and I will never be together, and I'm really clear about that. She needs to move on and so do I, so this call is not at all about her. It's really about Rory. I am on meds, and I have been seeing a counselor and I have been attending the chapel services and I see now that the main focus of my life is to become the father that Rory needs from me. That's my number-one goal. He has to have a dad who can give him what he needs or he's going to end up here, and I can't have that. With the help of my rehab and the pastor here, I'm really making progress, and I want to set up a time with Jessica where I can call each week or whenever she'll allow, so I can talk to Rory, just father-son stuff. I don't need to talk to her when I call. I just need her permission to talk to my boy."

"Well, I don't know what to say, Trent."

"Is she there?" he asked.

"Just a moment."

Mom turned to me, covered up the phone and put it behind her back. She looked at me with a shrug and a *Now-what-do-you-want-me-to-do* face.

"What did he say?" I asked in a whisper.

She reiterated everything he had just told her.

"How does he sound?" I asked.

"Actually he sounds *completely* different. I think he sounds pretty good. What should I tell him?" she asked.

I took the phone out of my mom's hand. "Listen, Trent. I don't trust you—I don't trust you *at all*. I'm glad you're clear that we are never getting back together because you're right, *we are never getting back together*."

"I know, I know," he replied. "I'm not calling to get anything from you. In fact I don't want to burden you at all. I just want to set up a time where I can call and talk to Rory. That's all I want. I've got to step up and be a dad now and he needs a father. The counselor and the pastor at the chapel say the same thing."

I stood there shaking my head—the absurdity of it all.

"Jessica?" he said.

"Let me just think about it," I replied.

"That's fine. But remember, I don't have any misconceptions about us being together. That's over and I'm good with it. I don't deserve your love and you didn't deserve what I put you through. And I want you to know I feel just awful about it."

"Call me here same time next week and I'll give you my answer, okay?" I handed the phone to my mom without saying goodbye and walked into the living room to sit down. My mom hung up the phone and followed me in, standing at the doorway.

"Now what are you going to do?" she asked.

"I don't know," I said quietly, staring out the window. "I don't even want to think about it."

"You don't?" she asked sounding surprised.

"Think about it? No."

"So you're not going to?"

"Maybe, maybe not."

"Well, you just told him you would."

"I know what I said, mom," I snapped back. "I just don't know if I'm ready for Trent to be a regular part of my thinking again, you know?"

Over the next week I vacillated between feeling that Rory should have some access to his father and being completely insulted that Trent would even ask. There was also the possibility that, if I didn't allow him to talk to Rory, it could set off his rage again. If he couldn't get to me, his brother Bobby was certainly capable of doing me harm. My mom thought the chance of Trent putting Bobby up to it was better than 50/50. I hated to admit it, but if I made him mad enough, she was probably right.

The day arrived that Trent was to call and I still hadn't made up my mind. It was just minutes before I was to expect the phone to ring, and I felt myself leaning toward granting his wish and allowing him to call Rory because I knew what it was like to be without a dad, plus I didn't want to live in fear of retribution if I told him no. At the same time, I felt angry with myself for it. The two sides of me were battling it out until the very end.

The phone rang. "Yes, I'll accept," my mom said. My heart raced. She handed me the phone.

"Trent, we can't keep putting Rory through all this craziness. It's got to be all positive from here on out. He's got to know that you love him, but he's also got to know that you respect his mother and mean her no harm. You've got to do everything you can to fill him with enough reasons for him to feel safe—to know that he is safe and so am I. Make him believe that everything is going to be okay because he has a dad who'll always be there for him. Can you do that?"

"So I can call him?" he asked.

"Trent, *can you do that?*"

"Yes, of course. That's why I'm calling you now," Trent said. "I don't really have anything in my life except for Rory. I have to get this right."

"Alright, look. Call here at this same time. We'll do our best to be here, okay?"

"Thank you. Jess, look, I just hope it's convenient for you."

"And this is a phone arrangement while you're in jail only," I said. "I don't know what visitation is going to look like once you get out."

"That's fine. I figured we'd let the courts decide all the visitation stuff."

"Okay. Anything else?"

"No, that's it. Thank you so much, Jessica. I have to go. I'll call."

My mom was listening intently as I handed her the phone. "He sounds really good," she said.

"We'll see," I replied as I walked away. Truth is, he did sound healthier than I had ever heard him before. And even though I didn't react to it, when he said, "I just hope it's convenient for you," it caught my ear. The old Trent would never have said anything as considerate as that. His whole life was about his convenience, taking whatever he thought he wanted or was owed to him, no matter what.

In the weeks and months ahead, Trent called regularly, and the calls all happened in the same way, with the same sequence. I would answer the phone, he would not ask me how I was doing but instead would solely ask me questions about Rory. He would then mention something he was learning about God or himself or what it meant to be a dad. Then I would put the phone to Rory's ear, who either said a few words or wasn't interested at all. At least Rory was hearing his dad's voice.

Rory received cards in the mail that I would read to him. They were always cute little thoughts followed by scripture from the Bible that Trent would handwrite in the corners. It seemed far-fetched that he was spending all that time in the Bible in order to create a false sense of security that would ultimately get me to drop my guard. I had to conclude he was really trying.

Four months later, Trent was released. My mom and I braced for an onslaught of harassing calls, but it never happened. He asked to see Rory and I made him available at my mom's for them to visit. He was considerate and kind to both mom and me. One afternoon he was tickling Rory and had pushed it past the point where it wasn't funny anymore and Rory was clearly in pain. I yelled at him to stop. He reacted harshly as if I had taken a tone with him that he wasn't going to accept. Initially, I viewed his reaction as proof that he was still volatile, and therefore, dangerous. But the more I thought about it, the more I realized it was probably just a normal reaction and that I needed to let him out of the fishbowl. Yes, it appeared Trent was becoming normal.

It had now been almost a year since he chased me, rammed my car and rushed the police station. I promised myself I would be cautious and ever vigilant. Yet I also found myself becoming more relaxed and at ease with my surroundings; the paranoia and constant awareness of Trent and the potential danger he presented was fading. One night after putting Rory to sleep, I walked to the front door, opened it up and sat down on a bench on the front porch under a lamp that illuminated me like a spotlight. I sat still and looked around but was not scared. I looked down the dimly lit apartment walkway to my left and then out to the dark parking lot to my right. Trent *could* have been out there watching me—but I simply knew in my heart he was not. Night after night, I protested the fear that I had lived in for so long, and I walked out the front door and onto the porch to sit under the light and declare an end to the cowering. And when the weather got warmer, I opened up the window and slept like a baby.

20

ENDLESS HUG

THE COURTS CONTACTED ME to say that because of Trent's history of domestic abuse along with his right to see Rory, we would be entered into a program where we'd meet to exchange Rory at a state facility created for just such cases. The estranged parents had to enter through separate doors at separate times and then exchange the child without seeing or talking to each other. It was sort of like an airlock at a space station, with two opposing atmospheric pressures never directly coming into contact. When I left the facility through my door after dropping Rory off, Trent and Rory would play in a brightly painted playroom with games and toys, and under the watchful eye of an officer of the court, who would provide an evaluation of what she observed. They had one hour to be together.

Rory would usually be in hysterics when I left him, but by the time I walked through my door to pick him up again, he seemed to have handled it pretty well. His eyes were clear, his face was dry and he was usually engaged with Trent or he was playing by himself while Trent watched. It all seemed to be going okay.

One day, Trent called to say that he wanted to return a document that I asked him to sign for the finalizing of our divorce. His hope was to give it to me when we arrived at the facility to make an exchange. I told him to leave it under the windshield wiper of my car instead of a face-to-face meeting. He didn't like that.

"Jessica, please don't make a big deal out of this. You're always making a big deal out of everything," he said. It was an interesting moment. At the same time that he should have understood where I was coming from, it seemed to also indicate that he in no way thought himself as a threat. I saw it as a good sign.

Still, the court-ordered visits were an exhausting dance that nobody enjoyed. I couldn't wait for them to end even though I didn't know what was on the other side. Finally, after six months, I received a letter from the judge's office saying that he was fit to see Rory apart from the facility and that the state was not going to pay for the service anymore. We were on our own.

Trent suggested that his parents' house would be a suitable place to make the exchanges. He had given my concerns a lot of consideration. He knew there were always plenty of people around—family, relatives and neighbors—and that was very appealing to me. I agreed to it. I told him that because of my job, it would be Saturdays only, with an occasional Sunday here and there. He was fine with that.

It was Rory who seemed to be the most on edge about this arrangement. I was surprised to see that after getting along with Trent fairly well at the state facility, Rory was often afraid to be left at Trent's parents' house. There were sometimes when Rory threw such a fit that I simply couldn't leave. I would sit there out of the way while they played, just so he could know I was there. But sometimes, in order to help Rory engage, I would find myself a part of the playtime. It was very uncomfortable: it felt like we were, all of a sudden, a family again. Very often, it would be me, Trent and Rory in the living room or out in the back yard by ourselves. I kept an eye on Trent to see if he was getting too comfortable with this new arrangement for visits; I didn't want him to assume too much, or really anything at all, between us. But he didn't. Whatever took place in the prison had a profound effect on him—the chapel, the counselors, the meds.

His family, on the other hand, didn't make things any easier. I'm not sure what I was expecting from them, but all they were able to give me was a brief hello when I would arrive. The rest of the time they would ignore me. I knew that deep down they were furious with me. At least they were kind to Rory. Sometimes Tomas, Trent's son with Maria, would be at the house. Rory liked having his little brother there. Our visits with Trent and his family were usually stiff and awkward, but certainly doable. There were even times it flirted with being pleasant.

My life started to resume some normalcy. I still kept my apartment a secret but could feel that my habit of checking around every corner was fading. I would go out with some of my workmates for dinner and even found the company of one gentleman to be enjoyable enough to make it a pretty regular thing. Nothing serious, but he sure was funny and cute. Yet even something as simple as laughter, I had to try on bit by bit. It was sort of like giving a dog slack on his leash—a little at first to see how it goes and then you can let it out more and more.

Did I deserve to be happy enough to laugh with abandon?

I was now a case manager for foster youth while working at the YMCA. It was hectic and crazy and relentless, but I loved it. I would wake up before dawn and get ready; then I'd wake Rory and get him ready for day care. I would eat as I fed Rory, now four years old, and then take him to Rebecca's house, the woman next door who also took her daughter to the same day care. I would try to be on the freeway by 6:45 a.m. to be at the office by 7:30 to get my caseload for the day. I would have a full day of visiting families with only 20 minutes in between to get from one to the next. It was grueling, but the work was important, not to mention something to sink your heart and hopes into. Good foster parents are unsung American heroes.

It was the kind of schedule that turned me into a walking encyclopedia of fast-food places all around East San Diego. I knew where everything was and because my salary was next to nothing and I was pinching every penny, I knew how much everything cost. Need a Wendy's? I could give you 20 off the top of my head. Burger King? Del Taco? Carl's? Taco Bell? Need a burger, fries and medium drink combo? Need a good chicken salad? I could tell you where the best one was and how much it cost down to the cent.

I was given a full hour for lunch but would use most of it to go over my cases so I would know as much about the families and the foster child as possible. I liked arriving at my foster homes feeling prepared.

Trent called and said that he had been working around town doing odd jobs under the table and had saved up a bit of money to help out with Rory. Up to that point, he had handed me only a few bucks here and there. I was grateful and eager to get it. I told him it would have to wait until our Saturday visit or when my schedule put me near his parents' house. I didn't have the time otherwise. He didn't seem to like that for whatever reason. But that's the kind of life I was leading. I was dead broke, and I still didn't even have time to go get free money.

At that time, one of our other case workers was on maternity leave, and the rest of us were going to have to pick up the slack—which meant I was about to get even busier. It seemed impossible to handle some of her cases and all of mine. One of her scheduled appointments was to meet and interview a potential intern. I was to meet the candidate at 1:45 in the afternoon for coffee about three miles from Trent's parents' house, so I called him to see if I could swing by at 1:30. It was the same day I had to run four other errands, including getting something for dinner that night as my refrigerator was completely empty. I needed that money.

I spent my last four bucks on a burger and water at a Carl's, reviewed a few case files and jumped on the freeway. I made it to Trent's parents' house at about 1:35 and parked at the end of the driveway among the usual array of cars that were commonly parked every which way. I ran through their weedy lawn to the dark brown house and knocked.

"Come in," I heard Trent say with a friendly lilt. I opened the door to see him standing on top of a chair replacing a light bulb in the hallway.

"Hello?" I said.

"Hi, come on in," he offered with a smile. He was such a different person now. He seemed lighthearted and smiled freely. Even the sight of him taking the initiative to fix a light bulb seemed to indicate a new man. When we were together, he didn't lift a finger. It was beneath him. Even so, I thought, *Good for him.*

I walked in and stood just inside the door. "I'm just going to stay here because I have to get on the road. But I sure am grateful for the money, Trent. If you could just grab it for me, I need to get going."

"Okay. Just give me a second. Come on in for a moment," he said breezily.

I looked around. "Where is everybody?"

"They're all out. Would you just come in and shut the door?"

I shut the door.

"How's it going?" he asked.

"Good, but super busy. Really, really busy."

"You live a crazy life, Jess. Would you just come on in?"

"I'm just going to stand right here, Trent."

He rolled his eyes. "Good grief, Jessica. Just come in for 20 seconds like a normal person and then you can go."

I didn't like the way that sounded, but then again, I didn't want to make him angry. I walked toward him as he stepped off the chair. He put a light bulb on the chair and a couple screws in his shirt pocket. He looked at me and smiled again and pulled an envelope from his back pocket. He moved toward me rather slowly holding it out. I hesitantly reached out and took it from his hand. It felt like bills inside. He casually opened his arms and moved uncomfortably close. "Give me a hug," he said. He put his arms around me. I stiffened. I returned the hug but just barely. I could smell alcohol. *Oh, shit*, I thought. I waited for a few seconds for the hug to be over. I let go of him, but he didn't let go of me. I patted him on his back.

"I miss this," he said. He held the hug some more.

"Nice to see you, too," I offered. "I really have to go." He continued to hug me. "Trent, please?"

He didn't move.

"Seriously, Trent. Can you let me go now?"

"Just hang on a minute, jeez," he said, continuing to hold me.

"Trent, please let me go," I said with a bit more bite.

Trent held me longer, only now a little tighter. He pulled my hips against his. His hand moved across my back, touching the back of my bra.

"That's enough now," I said. "That is enough!" Finally, I felt his grip ease. He looked me in the eye. The muscles in his face and eyelids loosened and sagged. Softly and slowly he said, "You fucking bitch."

In a blur, his hand moved toward my head, fingers spread apart. His palm collided with the back of my skull as his fingers clinched and created a fist full of locks. My hair pulled from my skin along my forehead and all around the crown on down to the nape of my neck. He pulled so hard my head snapped back, forcing my jaw straight to the sky, my eyes and mouth pulled wide. My back arched sharply and painfully. His other arm hit and gripped me tightly around my torso just beneath my breasts, pushing the air from my lungs. A sound came from my mouth with no words, like an ugly, guttural squeal. He put his nose to my cheek as he breathed against my skin. Like an animal, he smelled me.

21

PAYMENT

WITH MY NECK TWISTED sharply to the side, Trent pulled me by my hair straight down so that my knees hit the floor with a thud. He then dragged me into the den and threw me onto the floor. The couch was on my right. A condom was on my left.

"Trent? Trent? No!" I shrieked in disbelief.

He grabbed my face with his left hand and squeezed as hard as he could. "Shut up, shut up or I'll kill you." He mounted his 220 pounds on top of my small frame and straddled my left leg. He pressed his pelvis into the top of my thigh as he scissor-opened my legs. With his right hand he pulled violently at the snap and zipper of my pants and ripped them open. He pulled back and grabbed both sides of my waistband and pulled my underwear and pants off, with my legs going straight upwards. I was menstruating. He violently threw my underwear and pad out of sight. It was a disgusting mess.

"Trent, I'm begging you. I am begging you!" spilled from my mouth.

"I told you to shut up! Don't make me fucking hurt you!" He grabbed the condom and pulled it free of the wrapper with his teeth and a quick flick of his jaw. It had been nearly two years since we were together and now I was going to pay for each and every day. The look in his eyes was murderous.

He pulled my legs apart like he was trying to rip me in two. He forced his body in between and pushed his pants down with one hand, the other still squeezing my face. He put the condom on and plunged into me with violent recklessness. I began to scream through my disfigured lips. "Please, please, please!"

"You're getting fucked all the time by your boyfriend, right? Does he fuck you like this?" he growled. Like a piston, he punished me relentlessly. Tears streamed down my face.

Suddenly, there was a knock on the door. Trent stopped. We both sat wide-eyed for a moment. He felt me take a breath and pushed his hand over my mouth to keep me from screaming. "You better keep your mouth shut," he whispered, "or I'll rip your head off." We waited. I moved my foot from side to side to see if there was anything to kick. There wasn't. The person at the door, whoever it was, knocked again. Trent, in his panic, pushed his hand down on my mouth and nose so hard, I thought my teeth were going to crush into my mouth and my nose would crack and collapse. I was suffocating. My arms and hands began to flail. Still, Trent waited. The person knocked again. Trent kept his eyes on the door.

Finally, we heard the screen door close and the person walk away. Trent let his hand rise from my mouth and I gasped myself back to life. He resumed his quest. I couldn't move him, and with his hand over my mouth, I couldn't scream. I resolved to close my eyes and simply endure the onslaught until it was over. But the worst was yet to come.

Trent sodomized me from the same position. It felt like a sword was being driven into my body. I could feel the blood from my period all over the carpet. I tried once again to scream. He pushed down again on my face to keep me quiet, but the pain was too great to remain still. I squirmed, making the act a difficult one to complete. He tried for a few moments more until he placed himself back into my vagina. Like I had been accustomed to doing when we lived together, my mind transported me away to another place. Suddenly, I was on the inside of an island cave with a torrential storm raging outside. All at once, he moaned, and moaned again.

It was over.

He lay on top of me, sweaty and heaving. His grip of my mouth loosened. He absurdly thought my body was his to use as a resting place. I pushed him off. He flopped over and lay on the carpet. I sat up and leaned against the couch. "Oh my god. Oh my god," I said as I groped at my hair and wiped my face. He turned his body and looked at me.

"You seem mad," he said breathing heavily. I looked into his eyes—incredibly, they were absolutely, positively innocent of any misdeed.

"What?" I said incredulously.

With guiltless curiosity, he said it again. "You seem mad. You're not mad, are you, Jessica?" I looked at him with disbelief. "I mean, that was consensual, the way I saw it," he said.

"That's how you saw that? Consensual?" I asked.

"Yeah. I mean, you're not going to go tell anybody, right?"

I stared at him for a moment trying to understand what I was hearing. He was clearly unhinged from reality. I looked into his eyes again. It was terrifying that I was just inches away from a person who, with complete sincerity, lived in another realm, an upside-down universe that had almost no connection to the one I inhabited. I had to play it safe.

"Absolutely not." I said through a gravely voice. "I'm not going to tell anybody. I'm sure you didn't mean to do any of that, anyway. I know that wasn't you. If you'll just let me go, I won't tell a soul. Okay? I have to get to an appointment, so I'm just going to get going."

With tears still rolling down my cheeks and my nose running, I climbed over his body and gathered my pants and underwear.

"This isn't going to change anything with Rory and I, is it?' he said. "We're supposed to talk tonight at 5 o'clock. You're still going to have him call, aren't you? I'm not going to be telling anybody what happened here, so I hope you don't either. This was probably a mistake to do this, but at least it wasn't just me who wanted it, you know? I mean, I know you're not hurt or nothing, right?"

I didn't answer. I picked up the envelope of money and stuffed it into the pocket of my pants. When I found my underwear, I saw that my pad was gone. I had no idea where it was. I put my underwear and pants back on and noticed that my button and zipper had been thrashed and broken. I let my blouse hang over the front to cover it up.

"You remember what we said, right? No reason to go telling anybody about it," he said as I began to walk away in a hurry.

Before I got to the door I heard, "Hey, aren't you going to thank me for the money?"

I closed the door and sprinted toward my car.

22

THE NAKED DOLL

I GOT OUT OF MY CAR and walked quickly toward the diner. I opened the door and kept my head down so that I wouldn't have to look anyone in the eye. I walked straight to the restrooms. I opened a stall, sat down and tried to clean my bloody underwear with toilet paper and trembling hands. I pulled my pants up with a mass of paper between my legs and walked out of the stall to the mirrors and looked. My nose was red and runny. My eyes were puffy and black. My hair was every-which-way. My blouse was rumpled. My hands wouldn't stop shaking. My skin was pale except for what appeared to be a murky, red handprint on both sides of my mouth. I touched my teeth and nose, and they hurt. I had blood in my gums.

I put my palms against my eyes. "Oh, God," I said. "This can't be."

I did what I could to clean and straighten up, tugging at my blouse before walking out to find the woman I was to interview. There was a brunette seated alone and looking like she was there to meet someone. I walked toward her.

"Jill Pasqual?" I said.

"Are you Jessica?" she asked. She gave me her hand and a smile. I had no choice. I had to give her my quivering hand in return.

"I believe we can just seat ourselves," she offered. We found a booth and sat and chatted briefly; the windier-than-normal weather was the topic for the moment. I did my best to give her my attention and stay engaged. "Well," I said, putting a napkin on my lap. "Tell me about yourself." It was the last thing I remember, until I heard her say, "Jessica?"

I looked at her. I had just been replaying the horrors of the past hour in my mind. The pain. The suffocation. The humiliation. The incomprehensible conversation. My eyebrows were furrowed. My breathing was heavy. My jaw was tight.

"Jessica?" she said again. "Are you alright?"

"Oh, yeah," I said. "I'm just frazzled and tired, is all. I've had a crazy day today." She gave me a look. I could see in her face that she knew there was something more than that.

When we finally said our goodbyes, I walked briskly to my car and collapsed inside. I started to cry all over again. "What am I doing?" I said over and over with my forehead against the steering wheel. "Why am I here?"

I didn't have any idea what I was going to do and didn't even have a strong sense that I should do anything. It was as if time had stopped and all I could do was feel and have unrelated thoughts and questions pass through my mind.

Suddenly, as if on autopilot, I simply drove to the station, sniffling and gasping the entire way. I parked in the "visitor" parking space. As I walked toward the station door and passed by a few people, I felt they could tell what humiliation had just been done to me.

"I want to report a rape," I said to the attending officer.

"Oh, okay," he replied. He was clearly a bit taken aback. I don't know what I expected, maybe that he might offer some comforting words, or even come out from behind his desk and give me a hug. But he just looked at me for a moment. I wasn't sure what to do with my eyes. I felt them dart around. He was sizing me up. Was I legit or just another chick who had had a bad date? "Can you come this way?" He walked me to a nearby office, offered me a seat and told me that someone would be with me in a moment.

I called Rebecca and told her something terrible had happened and that I needed her to keep Rory. She said she would keep him until she heard from me. She assured me that he was fine to stay with her all night if I needed. When I hung up the phone, alone in the investigator's empty office, I cried in tall, towering waves.

Officers Taylor and Pappas questioned me for more than two hours, the goal being to determine whether or not I was assaulted or if there was reason to believe it was consensual or if Trent could have misread certain cues. When they were done and satisfied that I was telling the truth, they informed me that the next step was to take me to the hospital where I would be given the SART (Sexual Assault Response Team) exam. Before leaving the room, Officer Pappas, who seemed the most regretful of the process, informed me that he was going to get a pair of sweats that I was to change into. They would need to keep my clothes and undergarments for evidence. A few minutes later there was a knock at the door. It was Officer Hickam, the policeman who tried to convince me that Trent meant no harm.

"Ms. Yaffa?" he said tentatively.

"Yes," I said.

"I just want you to know how sorry I am for saying what I said to you, if you recall back then."

I nodded.

He looked at me for a moment. "I had no business opening my mouth like that. I was clearly wrong and I'm really sorry." I simply didn't have the energy to be forgiving at the moment. I stayed silent until he left. I burst into tears again.

I changed, and they drove me to the hospital where Karen, a SART nurse, was waiting for me with a gown and a warm smile. She offered me a seat and with great care and sympathy told me in no uncertain terms that what was about to happen would be awful.

For the next three hours, every inch of my body was examined, probed, swabbed, tweezed and photographed in painstaking detail—every bruise, tear, scrape, excretion and hair. She even opened my orifices to take pictures of my insides. Bag after bag, vial after vial was put onto a tray as I assumed position after position like a naked doll. It was the second indignation of the day.

After the exam, I was met by two new officers who once again interrogated me in the exact same way as before to see if my story had changed from earlier. They were satisfied that it hadn't.

I was more emotionally and physically wrecked than at any other time in my life. I walked out of the room where the officers questioned me as if being gently pushed forward by an unseen friend. I had nothing in me to do it on my own. I thought through all that was left for me to do on this day: drive home, get Rory from Rebecca's, put him to bed and then try to fall asleep myself. The only way that was going to happen was if the last vestiges of energy in my body kicked in and did for me what I could not. I kept thinking everything I was putting myself through was worth it. I believed in the promise: if I went through the legal process, I could put Trent away. And if I could put Trent away, I could put this whole nightmare behind me.

About nine hours after arriving at the police station that afternoon, a female officer drove me back to the police station. It was midnight when I got in my car and drove home with my head in a thick cloud of fatigue and disbelief. I knocked on Rebecca's door and woke her up. She let me in to pick Rory up off her daughter's bed. "I'll tell you tomorrow—is that okay?" I said moving quickly through her apartment with him in my arms.

"I'm just glad you're okay," Rebecca said as she watched me walk across the way toward my apartment. I remember thinking that I was about as far from okay as a person could get.

I opened the door, flipped on the lights, looked around, closed the door and lay Rory on his bed in a hurry. I hadn't yet heard whether the police had arrested Trent, so I checked every window and inside every closet just to make sure we'd be safe throughout the night. I climbed inside Rory's bed with him to hold him close, but after a while, had to remove my hands from around his body. They were trembling and ice cold.

Early the next morning, I received a call from the district attorney, Janine Hobart, who asked me the likelihood that Trent would call. I told them I'd bet my life on it. The police sent an officer out to my apartment immediately. He told me they would be recording any call that came from Trent and that my job was to get him to confess that I did in fact say no to his advances. Sure enough, as I had predicted, about 9 a.m. the phone rang. It was Trent.

"How are you, Jess?" he said with all the sincerity of a person looking only to save his own skin.

"Are you kidding me? After what you did?"

"You mean, what we did?"

"What we did? I didn't have much of a choice, did I?"

"C'mon."

"What do you mean, *C'mon?*" I said. "I didn't really have many options after you manhandled me like that."

"You wanted it too—don't fucking give me that!" he yelled.

"After I said no? Don't you remember me saying no?" I fought back. He paused for a moment.

"That was consensual, and you know it."

"Consensual? Are you crazy? Don't you hear when a girl is saying no to you? No means no."

He hesitated again.

"Is this call being recorded?" he asked.

"What, no! Of course not!" He had figured it out. He slammed down the phone, jumped out of his apartment and tried to get on the road but was quickly stopped by the police, who were waiting for him. He was arrested without putting up a fight.

My attempt to get him to admit that I did indeed say no was a failure and I felt awful about it. I didn't want to disappoint Janine. She was truly seeking justice for me. I also didn't want to ruin my chances for putting Trent in prison and felt that I just had. She assured me, however, that even without the recorded confession, we still had a great case.

"You've done the right thing, Ms. Yaffa. You've got nothing to worry about," she said.

I believed it. That was until I had my first conversation with Trent's mom.

∞∞∞∞

Why did you wince?
    I did? When?
When I said that if I put Trent in jail, I would be putting this whole thing behind me.
    That wasn't a wince. I definitely didn't wince.
Okay, maybe not a wince, but it was something. It was like a little something. I can't remember if it was in your eyes or your mouth.
    Well, if I did react, then I apologize. I try not to do that in
    my line of work.
It's OK with me, I'm just interested to know why?
    I guess it's always the same thing, you know.
What's that?
    A girl thinks that if her abuser could just go to jail, it will
    be put behind her in some way.

It's never behind her totally, is it?

>Never.

Wow. That's not good.

>What I'm saying is, it will never *not be there*. It will *always* be there. Victory over an abuser doesn't come when you forget it ever occurred, because that will never happen. It comes when you can use it to either better yourself or someone else, or both.

23

WHISPERS FOR THE PRIMA DONNA

I RAISED MY HAND IN FRONT OF my eyes like I did so many times before. The trembling was back, a cold quivering that I hoped would go away if I just balled my hands into a fist. Sometimes, it seemed to work. It would disappear for an hour or two, and I could feel my arms ease. I would look at the silhouette of my hand against the sky and feel gratitude for the stillness. I was happy that whatever stress was going on between my heart and my hand, it had been, at least for the moment, quieted.

Not the trembling in my stomach, however. That never left me. It would always be there in the pit of my stomach, an inner shiver that reminded me that deep down I was horrified. I could tell myself that Trent was in jail and wasn't getting out for a very long time, or that I was finally free of having to look over my shoulder. But none of that mattered. My body had its own understanding of the situation.

You're shattered, destroyed and scared to death, it said. *And there isn't a damn thing you can do about it.*

With my left hand, now shaking so hard I had to steady it with my right, I picked up the phone. I was going to call Audrey, Trent's mom, who, I was informed through a letter from Trent, was expecting a call. If nothing else, I wanted to maintain Rory's relationship with his grandparents and family however possible.

"Hello?"

"Hi, Audrey, this is Jessica," I said with fake calm.

"Uh huh."

"Trent asked me to give you a call and set up a time to bring Rory over."

"Uh huh."

"So just let me know what works best for you and I'll make it work out."

"Uh huh."

"So is there a best time?"

"Jessica, we wouldn't have to be going through all of this nonsense if you hadn't put Trent in jail."

"*I* put him in jail? Are you kidding me? You think he's in jail because *I* put him there?" I replied with anger in my voice.

"Why would you lie on him like that?"

"Lie? The evidence is all there. You know what kind of a person I am. Do you think I just suddenly made this all up? Why would I lie?" With her son in jail, I knew this wasn't going to be a pleasant conversation. But I didn't expect that she would assume that it was all a ploy to get rid of him.

"I don't know, Jessica—you tell us!" she bit back. "You're the one who went through the trouble of ruining his life!"

Suddenly I could hear Trent's sisters screaming in the background. "You lying bitch, Jessica. You know you're lying! You got to tell the truth now!"

"Hear that, Jessica? You've got some people mighty angry over here. You think you're going to get away with this? Well, you better think again," she said straight and cold.

"Am I actually being threatened?" I asked.

"If you got fear in your heart, maybe it's because you know you done wrong."

"Oh, really? You're going to sit there and tell *me* what happened? I don't think so."

"I know my boy ain't no rapist. I know you lied about him."

"You have no idea what the truth is."

"No Jessica, *you* don't. Hear what's in Jackie and Wanda voices? *That's* the truth!"

I had reached out in good faith. I had called to take Rory over to visit with his family. Now it was clear it was a toxic environment for him. There was no way he was going over there. It was done. I had made up my mind. "Audrey, I'm going to hang up. I'm not going to sit here and be threatened. And as long as you're going to accuse me and tell Rory his mommy is a bad person—which I believe you will, you can expect not to see him." I had just declared war.

By the time I hung up, the vibration in my stomach had revved up into a V8 engine. If Trent were acquitted, he would be out on the streets to get his revenge. But even if he were to be found guilty, I'd have his family to deal with. There were five of them and only one of me. It now appeared that with Trent behind bars, I was in more danger than ever before. Did I believe they would really hurt me? I was not only keeping Rory from them, I was keeping Trent from them—of course they would hurt me. It seemed to be that the outcome of the trial would determine who I was going to have to fear the most.

As the weeks passed, I had multiple meetings with Janine Hobart that seemed to be very productive. She thought I would be a great witness and reassured me that our case was solid. "So what you're saying is we're going to win," I said.

"I'm saying we have a strong case," she replied.

That, of course, wasn't what I wanted to hear.

The court allowed for me to be absent from the proceedings when I wasn't needed on the stand. It was a relief to know that I wouldn't have to relive a lot of the details. But on the fifth day of the trial, when it was time for me to testify, all hell broke loose in the courtroom. As far as Trent's family and friends in the gallery were concerned, I was a fragile, pompous butterfly making my way to the stand—the hated prima donna. They had grown impatient in the early days of the trial. After waiting to see my lying face, when they finally did get a glimpse of me, they broke out into a theatrical performance of silent stares, tisks, gasps and whispers. They did their best to look threatening, leaning forward and staring me down with squinty-eyed intent to harm.

When I took the stand, Trent turned into an eye-rolling, snickering mass of disbelief and incredulousness. Almost everything I said was met with the shaking shoulders of a person who had heard something so outrageous that he simply couldn't hold back the laughter. I guess I was naïve, but I had somehow expected that the proceedings would reflect the seriousness of the charges against Trent. Instead, it was a courtroom teetering on the verge of being overtaken by vicious clowns.

The defense attorney's strategy was to prove that I was a willing participant in the sexual act that took place in the Michaels' house that afternoon, and the reason my body showed so much wear and tear was because I liked rough sex.

Over the next three weeks, each time the defense attorney put me on the stand to testify, it was with the aim of embarrassing me. I had to give a movement-by-movement recreation of the rape and sodomy using wooden dolls to simulate positions. I had to answer endless questions about the unusually large size of Trent's penis. I had to recall every embarrassing word I had ever said to Trent about what I liked in the bedroom and ward off accusations about whether rough sex was my personal predilection. "The reason why no neighbors heard you scream is because you really like the rough stuff, isn't that right, Ms. Yaffa?" I had to overcome the cold, stiff dynamic of the courtroom and try to make the jury feel my hopelessness in those moments under Trent's control. Then, when I could finally leave, I had to walk out of the courtroom knowing that the 12 strangers on the jury would next be examining photographic evidence that revealed details of my genitals.

When I had started the trial I felt positive about my prospects for justice. By the end, just three weeks later, I almost didn't care. The courtroom was abuzz, the Michaels section was seething and taunting, and Trent was barely able to control his laughter. I had been destroyed by Trent, I had been destroyed by the defense, and what I heard from District Attorney Hobart was that the verdict could go either way. It was hard to fathom. After all I had been through, after his pubic hairs were found in my body and his DNA in the condom at the scene, after my bloody pad was found in the room where the rape took place—just like I had reported to police, and after the photographic evidence of an attack on my body, it still looked like there was a possibility the jury was going to see him as someone who simply engaged in rough sex with a girl who wanted it as much as he did—and he was going to walk free. Justice and common sense have absolutely nothing to do with each other.

On the days I wasn't in court, I lived with an odd sense that felt a lot like floatation. I wasn't happy and I wasn't sad. I didn't feel particularly fearful or positive. I was just numb, like I couldn't feel my own feet on the ground. I didn't have the energy to be upset or to even care. My goal was to simply hold on. I decided it was better to not let myself feel because to feel meant a loss of control, and I just couldn't afford that anymore. I couldn't let myself think about what was being said in the trial or how the proceedings were shaping the course of my life. I breathed slowly, smiled rarely and just tried to get from moment to moment. And when night came, I prayed that the gods would allow me to fall asleep when I lay my head down.

I was in my office after the final arguments were made to the jury when I received a phone call. "Are you sitting down?" came the voice of Janine Hobart.

"Yes," I said, my heart suddenly racing.

"Well it didn't take them very long to come to a verdict. Trent has been found guilty of all charges. You did it, Jessica. You put him away." I didn't say thank you. I didn't say anything. I simply dropped the phone, fell to my knees and cried. Suddenly, every emotion that I had been trying to keep at bay was set loose to rush through my body. It was an awful and glorious purging.

Trent received 29 years in prison.

That afternoon I went to my mom's house to pick up Rory. Her phone rang. "It's Trent," she said as she identified his number on the phone display.

"You have to be kidding me," I replied. She picked up the phone. "Hello, Trent?"

"Lillian, I'm on my way to prison. I want to say goodbye to Rory. Can I have a few words with him?"

I interrupted and took the phone. "Trent, are you going to have your family come after me?"

"Why would I do that?" he answered guilelessly.

"What do you mean 'Why would I do that?' Because your family is pissed off, and they would love to do it. All you'd have to do is say the word and I'm dead."

"That's crazy talk, Jessica. Of course, nothing like that is going to happen. They'll be fine. You'll be fine. Look, I'm really sorry I had to put you through all that in the trial. The plea deal they offered me was ridiculous. I had to go for it."

For a brief moment, I thought about pushing the issue that he knew from the beginning that he raped me, but suddenly I pulled back. Instead, not really sure of what to say, I just let out the rather meaningless, "I'm just glad it's over."

"So can I say goodbye to Rory?" he asked. I took the phone to Rory; they said a few things, and Rory either didn't understand what this goodbye meant or didn't care. Trent hung up, and then I hung up.

I stood there by the phone wondering if that was it. Would that be the last time Rory talked to his dad?

"Oh honey, aren't you relieved that he won't be a part of your life anymore?" my mom said as she walked past me.

"Boy, am I!" I said. "Of course! It's good to be free."

But I wasn't free. I looked down at my hand. It was shaking like I was gripping a buzzing alarm clock. Trent was still coursing through my veins.

24
Empty Girl

I DANCED. He stared.

Of course, he danced too, but it was merely so he could watch me twirling in the lights that were synchronized to the heavy, pulsating techno music. It's the only kind of music they played at *Hi, Society,* the nightclub that was nearly always pitch black, except for brief moments when it was illuminated by dashes of light from a strobe firing waves of blue and green into the crowd. It added a little peekaboo to what was already a game of cat and mouse. I bathed in the lights, the bass that passed through my body and in his hungry stare. He was really nice—nice enough to buy me a couple of sodas and carry on a perfectly lovely conversation, as lovely as one can get screaming over the music. He wasn't aggressive, just turned on. He was one more guy who couldn't resist the smile that would start small and then slowly grow across my face, igniting my eyes. My left shoulder moved ever-so-slightly forward and my chin would drop down so I was always looking up at him. It was as good as gold.

He would advance and touch me soon—they always did. He would grab me around the waste at my invitation—an invitation that began when I would pull my hair up to the top of my head and fan my neck. And there we would dance, arms around me, from behind, perhaps a little kiss to my neck. This particular guy was definitely coming home with me this night, no ifs, ands or buts about it. I knew him—and all the rest of them—like books.

But of course, this being the first night together, he wasn't going to get what he came for. He was going to get what *I* came for. It worked the same with all of them. They were going to get some loving, but just as much as assured me that they would call again, and they always called again. On the second date, however, they got the pleasure of my body in full, glorious gallops over the dunes of my bed sheets. It was exactly how I planned it. The cast and catch and subsequent sex felt good to me. It made me feel strong and in control. I laughed out loud and loved recklessly, deep into the night. I kept nothing from them, other than the fact that I was likely the saddest, emptiest girl on the face of the planet.

The brutalization I endured at Trent's parents' house exploded my already ripped-apart soul. I was left to try to overcome a grinding inside my heart, a gnawing sense that not just something but *everything* was wrong with me. I walked around with an unidentifiable ache somewhere inside. Nothing could reach it. No pill or mantra or meditation or wise quote or food or drink—nothing, except for one thing: Sex. Even though I had been told for years that I was a worthless shit—incapable of doing anything right—I knew it was my one exceptional talent. After all, I had done things that guys around my age probably never dreamed of or even heard of. It just so happened that sex was the one and only thing that also brought with it a high that, for a time, made all the aching and trembling go away.

That is why I danced or got gussied up to go to the store or post office or to the gas station. Men were out there in droves and I was going to use every one of them I could get to kill this pain. They were my only hope.

I had boyfriend after boyfriend with no time in between. In other words, the moment I told this or that guy to take a hike, I already had a new one waiting for date number two. There were no one-night stands; they did not serve my purposes. Each man in my life was its own temporary relationship. Relationships came with excitement and opportunities to get dressed up and see the wide-eyed look in a boy's face when he thought he might be on to something good. More importantly, new relationships came with a certain language. "You're so pretty, Jessica," they'd say. "You're the most beautiful girl I've ever seen. Your smile is so sexy. Not only are you hot, you're smart and funny." After all that I had been through, words like these were like water on dry, cracked land.

And I did not discriminate. I had black, white, Asian, Hispanic boys with regularity, tall and short, frumpy and put together. I had guys who took the bus to my apartment and others who picked me up in sports cars and whisked me off to box seats at the USC-UCLA football game. Some of them treated me well. Some treated me with a hint of neglect. None of the neglect, however, was a deal breaker for me. A guy forgets to call or show up for a date—and I was supposed to dump him for that? Another guy shows a bit of a temper because I can't let him come over one particular night—and I should have broken it off with him? After what I'd been through? These guys were angels.

But no matter how different they were from each other, they all had one thing in common: they were boys who needed a bit of fixing. Trouble finding a career? Problems with confidence? Anger issues? Feeling guilty for having such a horrible relationship with mother? I had lots of wise counsel that I dispensed without hesitation. But it got practical, too. They didn't have time to write their admissions essay for grad school? They needed a ride to the airport because they didn't own a car? They needed help picking out a suit and tie for an interview? I could do it all. "Jessica. I don't know what I would do without you," they'd say. "You're always there when I really need someone. I think you're the most amazing person I've ever known. I don't know how you do it. Even with a son and a job, you still have time to be so good to me."

It was pure, unadulterated worth.

And there was more where that came from. All I needed was a new boyfriend. So off I would go into the nightclubs, restaurants or the frozen food section of the grocery store. Time was of the essence because the sooner I had a new boyfriend, the sooner I would be flooded with all the things that gave me something to look forward to. Of course, when time is an issue, standards are not. Sure, here and there I would latch on to someone who was handsome and had a job. But if not, that was okay. It really wasn't them I was interested in anyway. It was what they could give me. So why waste time being picky?

After a while, however, I began to notice something inching its way into my soul. It was letdown. I felt an acute gloominess after giving my body away to these guys, not because I had a moral problem with it, but because the excitement I got from sex—and their reaction to it—began to wane. I had put so much into it, given it the keys to my healing and happiness, and suddenly it began to disappoint. They'd be in a drowsy-eyed heap of satisfaction lying on the bed with only enough energy to mumble how hot I was, and I would be in front of the mirror thinking to myself, *Aren't I supposed to feel a lot better than this?*

Still, I had no other options, and the churning deep within me was still there. I tried to fix the problem with longer relationships with men who were the marrying type. I got engaged to an investment banker who was an ambitious and charming wheeler-dealer. He cheated on me with a neighbor girl. Then I fell in love with a successful basketball coach who liked to talk about a future together as much as I did. I caught him making out with a cheerleader behind the bleachers. Things weren't going so well for me. They were about to get worse.

Rory, now in the second grade, was having a terrible time at school. He was loud, impulsive, constantly acting out in class, hitting classmates and driving his teachers crazy. He was diagnosed with ADHD. I spent some time volunteering in his classroom, and it was clear—he was acting on something deep within. I could see it in his eyes. My boy was deeply troubled.

One night, when I was getting ready to take Rory for a night out to meet up with friends from work, he came up to ask a question. "Will there be any brown people there?"

"Why do you ask that?" I said.

"Rory scared of brown people, mommy."

I looked at my dark, racially mixed son with kinky hair and thought to myself, *I have a problem.* The truth was, I had a plethora of problems. I was going to have to try to make Rory feel comfortable with all the parts of him that were connected to Trent, while in my own life, I was still trying to extricate Trent in every way—every memory, every wound, every bit of influence. I was in way over my head.

I was in the kitchen after work one night when it occurred to me that I hadn't seen Rory for a while. I realized that the shower was on and had been for quite some time. I ran back to the bathroom and opened the door to find a cloud of steam. I pulled open the shower curtain to see Rory sitting on the bathtub floor scrubbing his body raw and red with a sponge.

"What are you doing, honey?" I asked frantically.

"Nothing," he replied.

"You're not doing nothing! Look at your skin!"

"I'm scrubbing the brown off me. I don't want to be scary like daddy."

∞∞∞∞

Well it makes sense. I've seen it a million times in cases like this. Kids will have to deal with all that trauma some way. It's very understandable.

I can understand it, too.

Poor boy.

I kept hoping that all the stuff he saw would fade into thin air, you know? Most people can't remember much about their lives when they try to think about being really little.

It's got nothing to do with memory, Jessica.

Yeah, I know. You're right.

Even if he didn't remember a thing, it still shaped him. It's not just images sitting in his memory. It's really like an emotional, runaway train.

Wow. Heavy.

Think about it. Can you imagine being eight years old and knowing what look and skin color threatens your beloved mother the most, and it's you?

And I caused it.

It's a normal reaction to what he went through. Just like your reaction to what happened with your dad was normal, too. You really should stop assigning yourself blame. It won't do either of you any good.

Well, to not blame myself just lets me off the hook.

Listen to me. Let yourself off the hook.

25

THE MENTOR
BRINGS A WATERFALL

I SUPPOSE THERE COULD HAVE BEEN many other ways to approach Rory's fear of all things black other than to force a black man back into his life, but that was the best idea I could come up with. I wanted a black mentor for Rory.

I exhausted the phone book looking for organizations or programs that might have what I needed, but got nowhere. There were plenty of white female and male mentors, but at least in San Diego, there were no black mentors. I was out of luck.

I was writing grants for the YMCA as the director for prevention and education when I got an interoffice call. A different department was pursuing grants for a program that provided mentors to children of incarcerated parents. They wanted to pick my brain since my son fit the demographic perfectly. Toward the end of our meeting later that day, the team laid out the vision for the program, and I told them that

I hoped Rory could be considered if the program ever got funded. "Absolutely," they said. "You'll be first in line."

The grant process went smoothly and suddenly the program was underway. I filled out an application immediately and made my one request for a mentor very clear: a black man, *please*. There was one problem. They couldn't find anyone from the black community. To try and fix this, the YMCA hired a black man to become the recruiter to attract mentors from among San Diego's minority communities. His name was Joe Miller.

Joe's luck was no better than mine. The days were going by and he was getting nowhere. Each day he came up empty in his search. He began to fear that his lack of performance was going to threaten his job. One night after work, he sat down with a heavy heart and a folder full of applications and came across mine.

"Hmm," he thought. "Maybe *I* should do it."

Joe, 29 years old, himself grew up without a dad and felt the deficit of it his entire life. The more he stared at my application, the more he felt the desire to be Rory's mentor. His supervisor warned him against it, that it would be too big of a commitment on top of his other responsibilities. But he pressed the issue and ultimately got the okay. I was home the evening the phone rang.

"Hi, Jessica? This is Joe Miller from the YMCA. I believe we've met on a few occasions."

"Oh, hello, Joe. What can I do for you?"

"Well, I have your application here in front of me. I'd like to be Rory's mentor."

It wasn't until Joe said, "mentor" that I actually remembered who he was and what he looked like. He was tall and lean, straight-laced and soft-spoken with a large, dazzling smile that spread gradually across his face. I remember being impressed with him. I immediately thought about Rory, my little boy in a battle with himself, and quickly had images of him being proud and healed. My heart started to race. *Don't put any expectations on the man*, I thought, trying not to get my hopes up. Joe and I scheduled a time to meet and discuss the possibility. When we did, he said all the right things. "I don't want to just shoot hoops and play video games," he said. "I want to take him to the library, do homework together, do life together." He was thoughtful, clearly very smart and had the kind of refined manners that made him seem like he was raised in a palace. *Who is this guy,* I thought?

Before long, Joe came over to meet Rory and take him away for a day of fun. He took him to an entertainment park with rides, games and lots of ways to blow large sums of money. When they left, Rory walked out of the house clearly a bit miffed that he had to hang out with a stranger. But a few hours later, he returned with so many prizes in his arms I could barely see the smile plastered across his face. Joe was a smash hit.

And so began a relationship between Rory and Joe that I never could have imagined. I was hoping for something constructive and close. But what resulted was more like an all-consuming passion. Rory couldn't get enough of Joe's fatherly stature; for Joe, what started out as something he thought he should do, quickly turned into something he *had* to do. They loved each other immediately and quickly became inseparable. Joe's commitment to Rory was astonishing. No matter if he was sick, or having to take time off work, or simply too tired to add one more thing to his day, Joe showed up ready to take Rory out, help with homework or watch Rory's second-grade winter sing. Weekends were Rory and Joe time as they studied together and then went out to eat or got ice cream or played ball or watched movies or played video games. They had reached a father-and-son level of trust but enjoyed each other's company even more than most fathers and sons. We couldn't have been happier. I was especially happy—I could date all I wanted and never had to find a sitter.

One night, Rory and Joe invited me to go bowling with them. When I said yes, Rory was overjoyed. He held both our hands and beamed like a 100-watt bulb. I was getting tired of the guy I had been dating, and suddenly Joe, with his good looks and saintly patience and generosity, began to look very interesting to me. We were sitting together, and it was Rory's turn to bowl. As he stepped up to the lane, I turned to Joe. "You seeing someone?"

He almost choked on his pizza. "Uh, no. No, I'm not."

"Well, I think we should start dating. What do you say?"

He looked at me, like, *Where did that come from?* "Well, sure, I guess. That sounds fine."

"Okay," I said. "Then we'll start dating."

It was a good time for me. I had just been hired as the West Regional Director for a firm that offered drug treatment services to employees of large companies. And now, I had a new relationship to boot. Joe was always kind and considerate. He was the steadiest person I had ever met, calm and reserved, the perfect gentleman—always. And over the next weeks and months, that became the problem. For all Joe's kind and gentle ways, there was no drama or passion. He didn't shower me with praise. He didn't let me know I was driving him mad with desire. He didn't venture a grab when no one was looking. Nothing. Even when we had sex, it was so straight and by the book it was like we were stuck on idle. I thought, *OK, this guy is a major drip.*

At the same time, my new boss, Tommy, came out to San Diego from Philadelphia to conduct training. We spent a lot of time together, and one lull in our day found us talking about some pretty intimate things. He told me about how passionless his girlfriend was and how he could hardly stand it another day. He also told me whoever had me for a girlfriend was one lucky guy. Tommy had a powerful, stocky build, a bald head and a pair of clear blue eyes. He was rough and passionate and bad to the bone. He was a good 10 years older, but no matter, when he spoke, he seemed to be offering just what I was looking for—excitement. I knew with absolute certainty that our relationship was going to turn sexual. I knew I had to call Joe.

"Hey Joe. How's it going?" I asked nonchalantly.

"Good," he said. "How are you?"

"Good. Hey, listen. I've been thinking. You're a really nice guy, and I have enjoyed my time with you tremendously. But I'm just feeling like we're really not connecting, and I think we need to end our relationship. I absolutely want you to continue to see Rory, but as for us, we're just going to have to call it quits. I hope you can understand."

The line went silent.

"Are you kidding me? Why?" he asked with urgency.

"Well, I just said. We don't really have a connection, you and me."

"Yes, we do. We have a great connection!"

"Well, it's not one that I'm enjoying—so look, it's over. I'm not interested anymore."

He ended up getting off the phone keeping it together. The next day, however, was a different story. He called me with desperation in his voice, as if trying to keep a wave of panic from overtaking him. "Jessica, I bought you a gift for Valentine's Day and I want you to have it. I don't want to take it back and I don't want to give it to someone else. I want to give it to you. Please let me give it to you."

"No."

"No? Just like that? No?" he said trying to hold back the tears.

"Look, it's no. I don't want your gift."

"Jessica, please. Please let me give it to you."

"Well," I said, thinking it through. "Okay. I'll take it."

"Really? You'll let me give it to you?"

"Just drop it off at my mom's house and I'll pick it up the next time I'm there."

He lost it. He wept bitterly. It was the most emotion I had seen from him. "I'm sorry, Joe," I said. "I'm going to get off the phone now. See you next time you drop by to see Rory."

Meanwhile the emails that Tommy and I were sending each other would have made a sex therapist blush. Back and forth they went with unbridled sexual language and detail. I would break out in a sweat just to write them. I had to travel to a client in Utah and Tommy was going to tell the company that he had to fly out from Philadelphia and oversee my initial presentations. It was all a sham. We had planned to be together for one reason and one reason only: he was horny, and I was up for anything that might get at this gnawing ache that was still inside. I still had to find a way to get happy.

What began on that trip turned into six months of the craziest experiences I could have imagined. Tommy had one pursuit in mind—a sexual thrill, and he had no shortage of ideas on how to make that happen. We regularly had sex in public, frequented sex clubs, which were high-end orgies, had sex together with call girls, participated in web cam sex with multiple attendees and feasted on phone sex everyday we were apart. We carried on our romp all over the country with brazen recklessness. It was sick and exciting, and I never slowed down long enough to realize I was walking merrily along the sewer of existence.

Meanwhile I was getting phone calls from Joe's friends—even his mother—who pleaded for a second chance for Joe. "He's despondent. He's desperate. I've never seen him so depressed. He can't sleep. I don't know if he'll ever be the same. Isn't there any way you can give him another chance to show you how much you mean to him?" they would say.

"I'm sure I meant a great deal," I would reply. "But that's not the problem. I'm not interested, so please leave it alone!"

One friend called to say, "Joe's so hurt and lost, he's even going to church like crazy."

"Well, good for him," I said. "I hope he finds religion."

At the same time, Joe was also the life's blood to my escapades with Tommy. He would stay at my apartment to watch Rory as I flew off to meet Tommy everywhere and continue our pursuit for sexual thrills. Initially quiet and hurt after I had broken up with him for Tommy, Joe finally began to speak up. "Chasing this Tommy guy around the country isn't going anywhere, Jessica. This is bad, what you're doing." He seemed to know I was engaged in something very wrong.

"It's none of your business, Joe. Thanks for the advice, but you can just keep it to yourself," I curtly said back.

"Okay. But it's going to end badly," he replied. "You're going to get hurt."

At about the same time, I started noticing cards left for me at the house. Joe had begun leaving blank, unprinted cards that he filled with sentiments of love combined with bits and pieces of Christian messaging about accepting Christ and the love of God and His purpose and plan for me. It appeared that his submersion into his church had had a profound effect on him. But he didn't stop there. He began sending cards and Christian books in the mail all with the same themes of God's love and grace. Then came the emails—hundreds and hundreds of emails, some written at 2 o'clock in the morning telling of his—and God's—undying love for me. "I love you, Jessica," they would say. "If you just let God in your life, He'll help to heal you, and you'll see, we really belong together." At first, it was merely annoying. After a while, I started to get angry. I was receiving something from him every day.

I gave him hints that I no longer wanted his advances, no matter how shrouded in God's love and mercy they were. Then I began to get a little more direct about it. Still the notes, cards, books and emails kept coming. "Look, you! I've tried to be nice about it, but you just don't seem to want to listen. I don't want to go out with you and I don't want to keep hearing about your God! Please knock it off!"

"But I want you to come to church with me." He would say as if he hadn't heard a word.

"Hello! I'm Jewish—remember?"

"But Jessica, don't you see? I've forgiven you for what you've done to me."

"Hey, listen. I don't need your forgiveness. You're out of your mind."

"Jessica, look. You're a mess. If you just give God a chance, He can heal you and…"

"I'm a mess? Why don't you look at yourself and stop worrying about me, alright?"

"You just can't see it. But with God's help..."

And so it would go—conversation after conversation, email after email, Joe was relentless. The emails grew even longer, detailing all that God was revealing to him about himself but also about what God was revealing about Joe and me. Then he would end it with prayers for my protection as I flew with Tommy all around the country and for God to bring an end to that relationship, and for Joe and I to get back together. Then he would thank God for the joy that I would experience once I accepted His love. I wanted to pull my hair out.

Delete.

Delete.

Delete.

Delete.

Delete.

Six months went by, and nothing changed. Joe would come to my apartment and stay for days as I went from state to state with Tommy. When he would take Rory out, he would always bring me back a gift or dinner or ice cream. Sometimes he would just stop by and make dinner so that it was ready by the time I got home. I would just shake my head and roll my eyes. Even when he wasn't around, I found myself still shaking my head and rolling my eyes as if he had gotten so far beneath my skin that my disdain for him had become habit. I didn't want him anywhere near that level of consciousness. It had to stop. The next time he stepped all over my boundaries, I was prepared with the ultimate leverage: Rory.

It didn't take long.

"Here's a book I picked up for you, it's about how God sees marriage and..."

"Okay, look," I said, preparing to unleash. "I don't know how to say this any clearer than I've already said it, but here it goes again. Joe, look me in the eyes. Hear these words. I don't want your God. I don't want your Bible. I don't want your gifts. I don't want your cards or notes. I don't want your emails. I don't want your Power Thoughts (daily emails distributed to more than 2,000 people containing one verse from the Bible and two inspirational quotes that Joe would research himself). I don't want your flowers or dinners or desserts, and I don't want you! Can you understand me? Can you respect that? As a person, I have boundaries. You have stepped over all of them. You are making me very uncomfortable. Now stop it, stop it, stop it!" I put my finger in his face. "Are you hearing me?"

He looked me in the eye. "You're such a messed-up person, Jessica. I continue showing up here because God is telling me I need to, and you're hurting me and you're stomping all over me week after week, and I continue to come back. I don't want to keep coming back for more of this, but God is telling me to keep coming back. So I'm going to keep showing up, and you can say whatever you want, but for whatever reason, I'm called to be in Rory's life and in your life, and I'm not going anywhere."

"Oh, really? Really? Well try this on for size. If you don't knock it off, I will have to cut off your relationship with Rory!"

He dusted off my atom bomb like dandruff on his lapel. "I told you. I'm not going anywhere, Jessica. This isn't just about you and me. It's bigger than you and me." It was surreal. How do reason, pleading, anger, panic and threats mean nothing to him? Was he a saint or simply insane?

The next day I was at work and I went to use my company cell phone. It wouldn't work. I checked my emails. There was one from the national director. It read: *Jessica, you will find your company-issued cell phone does not work. That is because the jig is up. You've been found out. Call me.*

My heart shot up into my throat. I called him on my landline immediately. "Hey Jessica. Not good," he said. "Not good at all. You've been robbing this company blind for months. We've seen the emails between you and Tommy. They were brought to our attention by Tommy's girlfriend who, now I'm just guessing here, you didn't think was still in the picture. Anyways, he's been terminated. And effective immediately, you are also terminated."

I put the phone down and looked around the room. "Oh my God, oh my God, oh my God," I said. Tears nearly jumped from my face as I covered my mouth to keep the neighbors from hearing. I was devastated because I was guilty as charged. The shame was overwhelming.

I lost my job and Tommy in one fell swoop. About two frantic hours later, I got a call from Tommy: that girlfriend he said he dumped all those months ago, he never did. I felt like the dumbest, sickest fool anywhere. First I sat in stunned silence. Then I went and lay on my bed and heaved up and down as I sobbed. About an hour later, I picked up the phone, not sure of whom to call, just knowing that I needed to reach out to someone. But who? I came up with only one person.

"Hello."

"Hey Joe," I said sniffling and broken. "It's me. Have a minute?"

"Sure. Anything for you. What's going on?" he said.

"You were right," I said haltingly. "You were right about everything. I got fired. I'm probably in legal trouble with the company. And Tommy and I are over. You've been saying that I need to do some work on myself. You've been right about that, too. I'm going to take some time and do just that. I have to figure out why I keep attracting the same guy."

A couple of seconds went by. "I see," he said.

"So, I just want to say thank you. But I also want to say, uh, that I'm really so sorry, too—especially for the way I've treated you."

He gathered his thoughts for a moment. "I'm going to come over tonight. We'll work on your resume. I'd also like to contact some of my connections about you. Would that be okay? And let's not worry about your rent or your monthly bills. I'll take care of that."

I shook my head. "Are you serious?" I asked him.

"I've been serious about you for a long time, Jess. I'll see you tonight; try not to worry about anything. Okay?"

I put down the phone and just stared at it for a moment. I thought to myself, *Did I just confess that I blew it to a person who has been warning me that I was going to blow it, and still he didn't judge me?*

I don't think I had ever felt quite that low before. I was so devastated I didn't even have the energy to attempt to subdue the damn quivering in my heart. I didn't put on pretty clothes to go to the store. I didn't call my old workmates to join them at the clubs. I didn't think about men or sex or anything. For two months, I just let the ache do its thing. I just let it wash over me. I felt like my soul had the flu.

Night after night, Joe came by to see Rory and care for my every need. He was remarkable, but really, everything about Joe's character was remarkable. I had never seen someone offer that kind of love and devotion and get nothing in return.

I picked up some contracting work with some other agencies, and things were coming together, slowly but surely. And as they did, Joe resumed his ways. "I love you and I'll be here for you. If you'll just consider letting the love of Jesus in your life, you'll see that He is what you have always wanted."

"You aren't going to let up, are you?"

"Talking about Jesus?"

"And how much you love me."

"Oh. No."

"Joe, look," I said with exasperation in my voice. "I don't have the energy for this. Every time I talk to you about this, it's like talking to a wall, and I just don't have what it takes to fight you anymore. I don't know why you can't see that perhaps you have misinterpreted God's leading. I mean, it's possible, isn't it? I don't know how many other ways I can tell you this, but I do not love you, I do not *want* to love you, and I do not want anything to do with your God. For the one-billionth time, I am a Jew. I don't even like talking about your God, especially Jesus. So please, and for the last time, stop talking to me about your love and your God. I am begging you."

"Listen to me, Jessica," he said. "You've dated every turkey in San Diego, but you won't date me."

"I've already dated you!"

"Just hear me out. If you go on one lunch with me, just one, and you come away from that lunch and still feel like you don't want to be with me, then I will never say anything about it again. That is a promise."

"Are you serious?"

"I'm serious. Just one lunch."

"Hell, yeah, I'll do it. I'll do anything to shut you up."

"Great," he said and offered me his hand. We shook on it. "Tomorrow okay?"

The next day as I was getting ready for my lunch with Joe, I was steaming mad. This was going to be the most painful hour of my life. I wondered how many times I would have to say, "No, Joe. I don't want to, Joe. I told you I'm not interested, Joe. Thanks but no thanks, Joe." *What a joke*, I kept saying to myself.

He rang the doorbell at exactly 11:45 just as he said he would. "Oh, look who's right on time?" I said mockingly under my breath.

"Hi, Jessica!" he said as I opened the front door. I turned and rolled my eyes, not saying anything.

After walking down to the parking lot, he opened the door to his just-washed car, and I sat down with my arms folded over my chest. My *let's-just-get-this-over-with* disposition was in full display. He began to drive and carry on some blah, blah, blah conversation.

I looked out the window. The sky was blue, like always. The morning chill had burned off and it was mild and nice. There was nothing remarkable about this beautiful San Diego day. And that is what I was thinking as I was looking at the palm trees lining the road and counting the minutes to when we might be done. And that's when someone I didn't expect to change, actually started to. It was me. My eyelids suddenly got very heavy, as if I was all at once fighting to keep from falling asleep. Time started to compress. All the sound on the outside of the car began to go silent. My body became immediately relaxed as if I were losing control. All I could hear was that Joe was talking, even though I couldn't make out what he was saying. Each word felt like a warm raindrop falling on me—a waterfall of words. Everything felt so good and peaceful. I thought to myself, *This is nice. This is really nice.*

The next thing I knew, I was in a restaurant I do not remember entering, sitting at a table I do not remember walking up to, with food placed before me that I do not remember ordering. Joe was holding my hands and kissing me on the forehead as tears rolled down his cheeks and off his chin. As he kissed me and I sobbed, all I had the strength to do was to get out these words: "Thank you for waiting for me. Thank you for waiting for me."

I knew right then that I was going to be his for the rest of my life.

26

IT MEANS DADDY

I HAD ALWAYS BELIEVED IN GOD, but I never once considered He would break into my life and rearrange the pieces. Yet now He had. I had no way to explain what had just happened to me. All I know is that in one moment I hated Joe, and the next, I was secure about only one thing in life—that I would be his forever. How can anyone explain that?

On the way home, an elated Joe said as he drove, "I didn't want to even take you to lunch, but God told me, 'Take Jessica to lunch!' I kept telling Him that there was no way I wanted to put myself out there for you to hurt, but He just kept saying, 'Trust me on this one! Take Jessica to lunch!'"

It appeared that Joe's God was the kind that actually spoke my name.

"I've been dreaming of holding your hand in church on Sundays!" Joe exclaimed.

"Now, wait a minute," I replied. "Let's not get ahead of ourselves here. I'll go with you to one, but let's not start scheduling out all our Sundays just yet. And we're not taking Rory!"

"Okay. No problem," he said. "We'll just go to one and see how it goes. I'm just glad you're going to come with me at all."

I looked at Joe, who was beaming. He was animated and a ball of energy. I took his hand in my hand and gently rubbed the back of his with my finger. I thought to myself, *Am I going to wake up from this soon?*

I didn't *really* want to go to his church—it still felt like entering enemy territory. But I did want to know more about a God who would create someone I had the strong suspicion had been placed in my life to save it. "If this is the God you love, I'm interested in learning more about Him," I said. "I want to love who you love because I love you."

Joe took me to his church the very next Sunday. It was a huge venue, seating nearly 4,000 people, with large screens that flashed magnificent colors and images, artistic staging and a rock band that roamed as the lights pulsated. People raised their hands to this God, the same one that spoke my name, and they sang songs to Him wearing expressive faces, some with tears. It was loud, intense and deeply moving.

Then the pastor spoke. He talked about God the *Father* who loved us so much that He sent His son Jesus to earth to be the perfect sacrifice for us, so that we could be saved from our sins and enter into a relationship with Him, the *Father*. He was even eagerly waiting for us with open arms. All I had to do to have this Father was to believe and accept His Son into my heart. I don't know what I was expecting, but I wasn't expecting that, there in the middle of enemy territory I would suddenly feel like a little girl again, crazy, curly hair and all, feet dangling over the edge of my seat, wide-eyed and waiting.

I thought, *This can't be true.*

The pastor was putting a father figure, the one person I longed for my whole life, within arm's reach. I felt like I was 200 degrees. I was perspiring profusely. I knew for sure that he was talking directly to me. But how could he know who I was and what I had been through?

In the days that followed, I asked Joe every question I could think of about this Father and His Son, Jesus. It all felt so good—like I was falling in love on top of falling in love. I had never felt my heart being spoken to so directly before. Every word was like a breathtaking view from a mountaintop, then another mountaintop, then another. I had to go back to Joe's church again. I had to see if it wasn't just a mix up or a case of indigestion.

The following Sunday we were in our seats early. The moment the clock turned 10 a.m. the drummer, sitting under a bolt of light, struck his drum. Immediately it all came flooding back. People rose up, the lights began to pulsate and a mixture of fear and excitement filled my body. *Oh no. Here we go.*

Over the next four weeks, my thoughts were consumed with this Father. I felt myself in full-fledged want for Him, as if having Him in my life would somehow bring daddy home from work to walk past mom and Sam and into my room to take me in his arms.

And there, he would tell me he was saving up all his love for me.

It was a Friday night. The women's ministry was holding an event, including arts and crafts and a message—perhaps God the Father would be talked about again. I called Joe and told him that I was going to attend.

"Wow, all by yourself to a Christian church," he said gleefully.

"Some Jew, huh?" I said.

I walked into the event and could see that while there was every stripe of lady there—black, white, brown and yellow, tall and short, large and small, wealthy and poor—I still felt I stuck out like a Jewish thumb. But the ladies were beautiful, warm and friendly and I thought it was as good a place as any to change forever.

The senior pastor who spoke on Sundays was there again as the featured speaker of the evening. As he began his talk, I felt as though a small clearing formed around me, as if suddenly I were alone in the crowd because everyone had moved away, and a spotlight from overhead found me and fixed its lights on me. This was the pastor's message: Our earthly fathers fail us and fall short, but our heavenly Father wants to love us perfectly and unconditionally and is waiting for us, His daughters, to simply come to Him.

I put my hand in the other and raised them over my mouth. A new realization was making its way to my heart. I had been created to look to my father for my value; it's how I'm wired as a daughter. But whether my father is good or not, the final outcome is the same: he can't make me whole. He can be bad enough to hurt me, but he can't be good enough to save me. It suddenly left my dad with a brand new identity in my eyes: human. And if he was human, he was forgivable. In fact, he was easy to forgive. I could feel my heart begin to do it right then and there.

But there was more.

The pastor said that God the Father wants you to call him Abba, just as Jesus called Him. Abba means daddy.

I melted into a ball of tears. I could barely gain control. I wanted this Father so badly I could hardly stand it. The pastor asked if we wanted to receive Him into our hearts. *Yes*, I said fervently to myself. He led us in a prayer. I prayed every word along with him, my heart rising with each one. And there, by the power of Jesus' sacrificial death on the cross and His resurrection from the grave, I received my Father and received His love, at last. I had finally fallen breathlessly into my daddy's arms.

I began to cry aloud and didn't care who heard me. What concerns does a girl have when she's in her daddy's embrace? A life of chasing—and never reaching my dad was mine until Jesus held me close.

We opened our eyes and then clapped for all those who had accepted Christ. I knew what was going to happen next, having seen it over the weeks that I had been attending the church. He was about to ask all those who prayed the prayer to come forward. The applause was still ringing out in the room as I waited for the pastor to speak. It was at that moment that I heard a voice.

∞∞∞∞

Scars? Not many. I have a few things here and there. Probably the biggest, most noticeable one is my split earlobe.

    I wondered about that. You can't see it at all until you move your hair back.

Yeah. That's the only physical scar. I don't really care about it anyway. I mean I don't try to hide it that much or anything.

    That's interesting. Memories of the beatings don't hurt that much?

They're bad memories, of course—just not the worst, by any stretch. The name-calling is worse—by far. Every time he said I was worthless and stupid—nothing compared to that.

    I can imagine how that hurt.

Actually, it did more than hurt. He took away my sense of self. He spoke it so nonstop that he was beating my spirit right out of me, and that was just with his words. Then you start to become a believer—and that's when you've hit bottom because he's actually changing you, you know?

    Yes.

There were actually times when the physical beatings almost seemed to make some sense because in my mind, I wasn't worth anything anyway. I mean, who really cares? I think that's why the Gospel meant so much to me.

    You feel like belief in God repaired your self-image?

Not really. I was thinking of when Christ says, "Behold, I make all things new." I wasn't repaired. I was new.

27

A SOCIETAL NERVE

"EVERYTHING YOU HAVE been through, I'm going to use to bless others," the masculine voice said. I looked around to see who might have said it. I looked behind me. I saw a row of women still clapping. It couldn't have been one of them.

"Everything you've been through, Jessica. I'm going to use to bless others," I heard it say again. I ventured another quick glance around to find where the voice might have come from. There wasn't a male in sight.

I gasped. "Is that you, God? Are you talking to me?"

The next thing that I knew, as if carried away by a current, I was at the altar on my knees, praying as the pastor led. I don't recall getting out of my row, nor do I recall walking there. The only thing I was sure of was that something amazing had just happened. Maybe everything amazing had just happened. I had just accepted Jesus as my Savior and was spoken to—even given a purpose for my life—by God Almighty in the same moment.

Even so, I still managed to unleash a wave of fear on Jenna, the altar-call volunteer who came to my side in the altar-call room. "I'm a Jew, and I don't know what I'm doing and what if my mom freaks out and I'm going to need help to actually be a Christian."

"You don't have anything to worry about," she said. She touched my arm in a comforting way.

Through tears I looked at her as if to say, *Okay, are you going to tell me why not?*

"We all come to God with our stuff, you know?" Jenna said. "It could be our religious upbringing or our history or our sin or our emotional baggage or just plain fear—or whatever. Just as long as you come—that's all He wants."

I was happy to hear that.

"Why don't you meet me at a Bible study I go to? We're just a bunch of young ladies just trying to work out our faith. You should come!" Perhaps I had never felt hopeful before in my life. Because at that moment, the hope I felt didn't even seem remotely familiar.

Joe was at a diner with Rory when I called. "I did it! I did it!" I screamed into the phone. "I accepted Jesus into my heart!"

"Oh, babe, I'm so happy for you, for me, too. I've dreamed of this for so long!" he said with his smile coming through the phone.

"I know, I know." I replied. "What do we do now?"

When Sunday came, we went to church, but for me, it was really like going home. I stood along with the others and raised my hands and let the tears flow. I was just like everyone else. I was an orphan now a part of a family.

Monday morning came, and I got on the church's website to find a ministry that I could offer my help to and honor the Voice who, I knew in my heart, was God. Of the more than 100 ministries that this church supported, not one of them was there to address victims of domestic violence and sexual abuse. When talking to the woman who headed up the Care and Concern ministry, she told me that the number-one call that came into that department was from women who wanted to leave their abusers or just had. All the church could do was direct them to outside, secular sources. I felt a strange pressure on my heart. "Oh, no," I said to myself. "Not me, Lord."

When I got to the Bible study, Jenna was waiting for me. I joined in with the rest of the ladies and soaked up every word and emotion that these lovely women expressed as they told their story. Each time when I left the Bible study, I couldn't wait to go back. After four meetings, I too, felt comfortable enough to tell my story. Another woman there, Nicoletta, who had sat rather quietly up to that point, stepped forward and revealed that she was a survivor of rape. She also added that when I spoke about the Voice after I received Christ, she felt absolutely certain that it was God who spoke—and one more thing: She was equally certain that *I* was the one to start a domestic violence ministry.

Uh oh.

Everything was lining up. People were starting to look to me. Even though I had no desire to start a ministry, I was feeling clearer about the calling, and the need was definitely there. A couple of weeks later, I could deny it no longer. I made the trip to church, asked for an application to start a ministry and sat down to fill it out. It was a surreal moment. There I was, a Jewish girl who, until a few weeks before had never stepped foot inside a protestant church. Now I was about to start a ministry based on the life and teachings of Jesus Christ. I could hardly believe it.

The entire process, including meetings, interviews, providing additional information plus lots of phone calls with the director of outreach, took just more than three months. It was plenty of time for me to swing back and forth between stalwart belief that I was being called to the ministry and total conviction that I had absolutely no business doing what I was about to do. Sometimes I felt strongly that

God was leading my path at the same time I was calling out to Him to remove it from me. When the final approval came, it was like a gift *and* a dagger to the heart all at once. "Oh, crap." I said.

Nevertheless, three weeks later on a Tuesday night, after putting a tiny ad in the church bulletin two Sundays before, a volunteer and I met at 6:45 p.m. to pray and conduct the first Domestic Violence ministry meeting. We were assigned a small room on the 2nd floor, and we had the facilities guys supply us with 10 chairs that we made into a circle. "Oh, Lord," the volunteer prayed as we held hands, "we know there are so many who are in need of a touch from You for all the pain and agony they are experiencing at the hands of their abuser. Heavenly Father, please, move mightily in this room tonight. Bring us the women to fill these chairs so that we may fill them with hope—Your gracious and powerful hope. In the name of Jesus we pray, Amen."

As we looked up, a woman came through the doors. Then another. Then another. By 7:05, 68 women had crowded our little room. I had to call the facilities guys and put them on the task of finding somewhere bigger for us to go. I felt like I was filled with helium. God spoke to me on the day of my conversion and was still speaking.

I sat there with 68 beautiful faces of every type looking at me. They had just walked out of the nearby neighborhoods to come and be helped through their pain, to be offered a little hope and healing—and they were looking to me to provide it. I just had to take a moment to stare back. It was clear as I looked into their eyes, this ministry was filling a desperate need, and this was just the beginning. A societal nerve had been struck.

28

PEGGY, RHONDA AND THE POWER THOUGHT

THE MINISTRY SPREAD LIKE wildfire. Women were coming from every corner of San Diego and beyond. I was on my heels immediately. I had never anticipated the volume of women who were desperate for help.

Two women from the church, Peggy and Rhonda, came alongside me and bolstered my efforts to offer the love of Christ to these women. I was grateful—at first. Soon, they began to try to mount an argument as to why the leadership really shouldn't be in my hands. They hinted to me about it. Then they came right out and said it. "Why should you be the leader?" they said. "You don't know near as much as we do. How can you be the leader when you have been a Christian for just a few months? We've been Christians for many, many years. What do you know of the Bible? We've studied the Bible all our lives. We don't understand why our names are not prominent on the website. Why only you? Why haven't you consulted us about what the site will look like?" Then they appealed to the church leadership about it. Soon they were talking to the ladies in the support group about it, trying to get some of them to seek them out rather than me. I was barely keeping my head above water as it was, working full time, raising Rory, leading a ministry and trying to carry on a relationship with Joe. Peggy and Rhonda's aggressive pursuit to bring me down was more than I could handle.

I was pushing back at their efforts to topple me, but at the same time, I wasn't entirely sure they were wrong. Even so, the church leadership assured all of us that they were solidly behind me and that they had come to their decision about leaving me in the leadership position through much prayer. Still the tug-o-war with Peggy and Rhonda continued. Four months went by, and while they were absolutely pivotal in handling everything that I could not, such as all the crisis-call management—which was huge and needed experienced people—they were killing me at the same time.

It was at this time, Shawna, a young lady who was in the group for her own healing, stepped forward to volunteer her time. Rhonda got on Shawna's case about the way she handled a moment of crisis for another woman, and it hurt Shawna to the core. She came to me to say that she was an emotional wreck after what Rhonda had done and after all she had just endured at the hands of her husband, she didn't know if volunteering for the ministry was the best thing for her.

I called a meeting with Rhonda. "Listen, I am going to require that everyone who volunteers here feels safe. Whether Shawna was right or wrong about how she handled the situation, it doesn't matter. Your approach in handling her made her feel unsafe, and that is unacceptable."

"Who do you think you are?" Rhonda said, indignantly. Before I could answer, she grabbed her things and left, never to return.

At the exact same time, Peggy had decided to move away from San Diego. I was finally rid of the constant struggle to stay on my post as leader. But here was the problem. I was absolutely alone.

It was then I made a critical mistake. I allowed myself to believe that because God had placed me in the position of leadership, He must be equipping me to perfectly handle any and all situations that came my way. I took every phone call. I handled every crisis. I got a roof over the head of every woman, fed every child who needed food, saw that every woman who needed counseling had somewhere to go, talked to every woman who needed one-on-one time after support group. Soon, as I began to feel the wear and tear of that kind of pace, I questioned what kind of leader I could possibly be if I couldn't get the job done. After all, each situation was life or death. If I couldn't do my job, someone could get killed. If my phone was ringing, I figured God was intending for me to help the woman on the other end of the line.

Meanwhile Joe was the loving and long-suffering partner that I never dreamed I would have. The graciousness and generosity that he displayed prior to us getting back together was not simply an attempt at winning me over. It truly was who he had become. Even though Joe was playing second fiddle to the ministry, he was supportive and remarkably patient and understanding. I was the luckiest woman around. If only I had the time to enjoy him.

It was a Friday night, the eve of my 32nd birthday. I arrived home around 10 p.m. and dragged myself into the apartment, where Rory and Joe were finishing up a movie.

I dropped my bags. "Hey, do me a favor, will you, Joe?"

"What's that?"

"Spend the night so we can wake up in the morning and have breakfast together—you know, for my birthday."

"Oh, sorry. I can't."

Joe would take the couch on a whim. I never once had to ask him twice. Yet this time, on the eve of my birthday, he was turning me down.

"Why not?"

"I got stuff to do."

"Stuff—what kind of stuff?"

"Just stuff, is all."

"Oh, okay," I said, a little miffed.

"But keep the day free. I have plans for your birthday," he said.

"Okay," I said. I thought to myself, *That was weird.*

Joe hugged Rory, gave me a kiss, and then walked out the door. "See you tomorrow," he said with a glint in his eye. I said goodbye and shut the door behind him; I leaned against it thumbing through everything that just happened. *Why wouldn't he stay?* I wondered. *We could have all gotten up really early so he could still get to where he had to go.* Then it dawned on me. I started to squeal with excitement as I put my hands over my mouth.

"What's going on, mom?" Rory wanted to know.

"I think Joe's going to ask me to marry him tomorrow!"

We jumped around and danced and hugged. We were both out of our minds with excitement. I got on the phone with my mom and as many girlfriends as I could think of to lay out the pieces of tonight's conversation with Joe so they, too, could confirm that yes, he was going to propose.

They all agreed with me—a proposal was coming. I went to bed that night smiling so broadly my face started to hurt. "Thank you, God!" I shouted in the dark. "I love him so much!"

I was up early the next morning, anticipating all that Joe had planned for me that day. At about 8 a.m., I got a text. "Check your email," it said. I ran to my computer and flipped it on. There was only one email. It was from Joe. The subject line read: Today's Power Thought.

Hmm. That's odd, I thought. *Joe never does Power Thoughts on the weekend.*

I opened it. It read:

Dear friends and family, I am sorry to disturb you all on the weekend, and as you can see this is not an ordinary Power

Thought—because this is no ordinary day. I wanted you all to know that this is the birthday of the special lady in my life. So I thought it was fitting to surprise her this way—because she loves Power Thoughts :)

Once upon a time, two people met, thought they had true love, but eventually broke up. Then God brought them back into each other's lives when He felt they were right for one another. She was beautiful, caring and loving, and she had a son, whom the man also fell in love with. The man was so overjoyed when God brought them back to him. To show his appreciation to God and her for bringing him such joy, he wants the young lady and her wonderful son to follow these instructions today:

First go to our favorite place to hike—the highest trail that we have never walked up. You know, the one that gives you a view of the whole city like you are sitting on top of the world? I want you to meet me right there, and as you're walking along the trail getting higher and higher, I want you to think about us and how far we have come. Think about your many blessings in life, the struggles and heartaches but how you believed that in the end it would all work out for good. And it has.

I want you to think about how much I love you and how I want to share it with the world :) Are you the girl in the fairytale? If so, please stop reading this and come quickly to the top of San Elijo Mountain. I am waiting.

In a blur of grey cotton, I threw on a pair of sweats and a sweatshirt, told Rory to jump into his tennis shoes and grabbed our dog, Marshall. I broke every speed limit as I screeched through the streets of San Diego under a beautiful morning sun and tore on down to the bottom of San Elijo Mountain. "Let's go, let's go, let's go!" I barked as I, like a fool, began to run up the face of the mountain. With my cell phone in hand, I began to call everybody I had called the night before and tried to tell them about the Power Thoughts email while I was huffing and puffing. Nobody could understand a word I said, but they all agreed—this was exactly what we thought it was.

"Mom, wait up!" Rory called from behind.

"Get your butt up here!" I yelled back, gasping for air.

We passed by the spot on the mountain that we had climbed to before but couldn't go beyond because of fatigue, and I was still running.

"Mom, please!" Rory yelled.

"Nope!" was all I could get out.

I was sweating like a horse as my boots dug into the mountain. My lungs were stretched to their limit.

"There he is! There he is!" I heard from behind as Rory called out.

I stopped to look. Joe was standing atop the mountain, arms outstretched. I felt myself welling up. "I'm coming!" I yelled out. "I'm coming, honey!"

When I got to the top, I stumbled into his arms, and there we held each other. He looked into my eyes and kissed my sweaty face. "Happy Birthday, my love," he said.

The view from the top of San Elijo Mountain was spectacular, with all of San Diego and the ocean beyond in view. It beamed like a golden city. After a time, he said, "I have something for you."

"You do?" I said trying to act like any gift was a gigantic surprise. He handed me a small bag. I looked at his face, and he was aglow. I looked inside. There were three tickets. They were to a brunch at the House of Blues.

"Oh, hey, wow!" I said, checking the bag again to see if there was something I might have missed at the bottom.

"We always said we wanted to go there, so, we're going to go. Tomorrow!"

"Oh, hey, wow," I said again, trying not to let my disappointment show. "That's…so…great!"

"Aw, I knew you'd like it," Joe said as he hugged and kissed me again.

"Yes, of course I do," I said with a big broad smile. *What the crap!* I thought to myself. Now I have to call everybody and tell them that I was totally off! His big surprise were tickets to a brunch!

Joe, Rory, Marshall and I walked to the far end to get another view. I walked just a bit ahead, still panting, and tried to give myself a pep talk that I shouldn't be disappointed. *Don't let it ruin your birthday,* I kept saying. Then all of a sudden, and for no particular reason, I turned around.

Joe was on top of a large rock on one knee holding a small box. I immediately began to cry. "Come here," he said. As I approached, he motioned over to the side. There was a tree nearby with, WILL YOU MARRY ME, carved into the wood.

I gasped and put my hands to my mouth. "When did you do that?" I asked smiling from ear to ear.

"This morning. I've been up here since 5:30," he replied, also beaming.

"But the Power Thought. You sent it at 8 o'clock."

"I had Andy send it from his computer."

"But I don't understand—"

"Jessica! Will you?"

I looked at Joe's handsome face with his proud smile. He knew he had done something really good.

"Will you marry me and turn us into a happy family?"

"Yes!" I said, breaking into deep sobs.

Rory let out a, "Woohoo!" and ran to us as we all hugged and cried with Joe still kneeling on the rock and Marshall barking and flipping out.

"We love you, Joe! We love you so much!"

"I love you, too." Joe said, his voice cracking and his eyes welling up. "I have to get up," he added. "This rock is killing my knee."

29

FLINCH, TURN, RUN

THE SUN WAS SHINING down on me like no other time in my life. I was being used in significant ways to meet the needs of women living through abusive relationships and I was going to be married to the most wonderful man I had ever known. It was a golden era.

What I couldn't understand was why there always seemed to be a little grey cloud floating across my horizon. Sometimes I would be going happily through my day, and all of a sudden, a slight feeling of sadness would waft through my mind that I couldn't look up in time to fully see. The little grey cloud had appeared, ever so briefly, in my periphery.

I had become the picture of purpose and significance and it felt wonderful. I had the love of my Father in heaven. I meant the world to Rory and to Joe, and the list of women who also felt that way about me was growing longer every day. Even my work life was spectacular; I was needed and even admired. What could be more wonderful than true worth? I was working hard—harder than ever before—but that was okay. When there is so much importance attached to your life, hard work feeds the soul. If only I could have given that nagging, little grey cloud the slip.

Meanwhile, the steady flow of women into the ministry plus the lack of experienced help necessitated that I heap nearly all of the weight of every crisis onto my own shoulders. I was working 16-hour days to make sure everything was done impeccably. Being with Joe only here and there left me an emotional mess, and while it would have made sense that seeing him so sparingly would cause a feeling of emptiness, that didn't seem to be the reason for the little grey cloud. But what was it?

More and more, I felt something was wrong but was unable to explain it. I looked in the mirror. "What's wrong with you?" I would say to myself. "Why can't you just be happy?" I was helping abused women find shelter and start new lives. Their children were being fed and protected. Their husbands were having to look themselves in the eye and decide if this was the life they really wanted to lead. My mom, Lyndi and Joe were busy handling wedding arrangements when I couldn't, and it all seemed to be going smoothly even in light of the wedding date being only three months away. Still, the feeling of sadness was there. My body started to feel depleted. "I know, I know," I yelled at myself. "I'm tired. I got it. I'll take a day off." I tried to convince myself that no one could keep up this pace, and the way I was feeling was to be expected. But deep down, I knew I was lying to myself. I looked up again. Suddenly, the little grey cloud wasn't so little any more. It was a dark, threatening cloud, large and as still as night.

My emotions were bone dry and brittle. I could be set off in a moment's notice, either into tears or rage. I could barely pull myself out of bed. The calls from women-in-need kept coming. Moments with Joe kept leaving me drained. I felt panic rise in my body. I tried to inhale and exhale it away. "Lord, there are too many ladies," I yelled out. "What am I supposed to do?"

Thoughts of my past floated through my mind at an alarming rate. "Why now? Haven't I moved on? Didn't I experience healing?" I said to God. "Why do I feel like I'm being buried alive by everything that has happened to me?"

It was a Tuesday morning. The alarm clock went off and my eyes struggled to open. I knew had to get Rory up to go to school, but I wasn't moving. With one eye, I periodically looked at the clock. It was getting late, but I still wasn't getting out of bed. I knew what was at stake; if I didn't get Rory up, he would be late and in trouble. Still, I didn't move. I couldn't. About 30 minutes later, Rory walked into the room, rubbing his eyes. "Am I going to school, mom?"

I pulled myself up like I had a sandbag on my chest. "Go, baby. Get dressed. I'm sorry," I said with a scratchy voice. I went to the bathroom, stepped into my slippers, put on a robe and drove him to school completely as is. I stumbled back into the apartment, kicked off my slippers, lay down on my bed and called the director of ministries at the church. I left a message. "I'm in crisis," I said. "I won't be taking calls." Soon after, I got a text back: "We'll handle it."

I flipped off my phone and lay my head back down. Was the thunder and rain that I heard outside something I was imagining? "Uh oh," I said to myself. For the next three weeks, I barely moved. With my hair pulled to the top of my head, I lay in my pajamas and rarely ate, drank or even slept. I moved very little, lying flat on my back, looking up at the ceiling. I would get up to go to the bathroom and then come directly back and lie down. I would drive Rory to school and had a friend bring him home, but I did not feed him; I was simply unable. He prepared all of his meals himself, which were cereal, sandwiches and macaroni and cheese. I didn't shower. I didn't brush my teeth. I didn't talk. I didn't watch TV. I didn't pick up around the house. I simply looked around, occasionally slept, and frequently cried.

My lungs would heave up and down as if I were unable to get oxygen. It made me cry harder, which made my shortness of breath even worse. At a moment's notice, my heart would race so loudly and violently I was sure Rory could hear it on the other side of the wall. I thought I might never leave my room. Worse yet, I thought I might be dying or going crazy or both.

Joe would call, and I would tell him I was sick and then try to get him off the phone. The more I thought about the wedding, the more despairing I became. The more I thought about the women who weren't receiving my help and still living with their abusers, the more sick I felt. Finally, it became clear that a perfect storm had converged and that my soul was the point at which the storm clouds collided. I was worn to the nub by the ministry, which prohibited any defense against all the emotions that were triggered by the idea of marriage. All I knew of marriage was pain, judgment, isolation, failure, accusation, as well as emotional terror and physical beatings. There was no way to convince myself that was not going to happen with Joe. Self-pep-talking didn't amount to even one constructive thought. It was all just psychobabble. My body was the holding place for all the trauma I had experienced, and now that I was about to be *married* again, all my nerve endings were telling me to flinch, turn and run.

Yet, my fear was two-fold: I feared what Joe might do to me based on what I knew of husbands, and I was also afraid of what it was going to do to him when he learned everything about me. The ways in which I could disappoint him were many and spanned everything from the puny to the profound. I wasn't pretty in the morning. My hair was tougher to deal with than I had ever let on, curlier and rattier too. I wasn't a great cook. I wasn't neat and tidy like he wanted. We couldn't be sure that none of the abuse wasn't going to come back to haunt us both. What about my sexual past—how might that cause a wedge? What would we do then? I felt like a burning cauldron of seen and unforeseen trouble and problems that left no options but to one day make him run for the hills.

Finally Joe, annoyed by my disappearing act, called with urgency and demanded answers. "What is going on over there? Why can't I see you? Just how sick are you?"

"It's just that…I need some time," I said with barely the energy to get the words out.

"You've had three weeks. What is really going on?"

"I think we may need some space," I said, crying.

"What? Honey, please. Let's talk. Please don't keep me in the dark any longer. What on earth is going on? I'm coming over!"

"No, Joe, don't. I beg of you not to come over. I won't let you in."

"Babe, please. I can't go through this anymore. I love you. Whatever you're going through, we'll get through it."

"I love you, too, but I'm not sure this is right. I'm not sure we should be trying to make this happen."

"Are you talking about calling off the wedding?"

"I don't know. Maybe. Yes."

"Why? I don't understand."

"I just don't think I can make you happy. What if I'm not what you expect?"

"You have got this all wrong, honey. Our wedding is in six weeks. You're just getting cold feet, but it will be fine. Please, don't let yourself go down this path. I'm begging you."

I sniffled in the phone. "There's just so much you still don't know. I'm just really scared of what you'll think of me if you really know all of me."

"I'm excited about it, babe. I have a lifetime to learn everything about you. What could be more exciting than that?"

I thought about it for a moment. I was making this wonderful man suffer.

"Just give me a few more days," I said. "I'll call you, and we'll get together and talk, I promise. Just give me a few more days. I'll figure some things out by then."

I got off the phone, pulled myself up off the bed, went to the computer and searched: counselors, trauma. The first name that came up was *Anne Thompson.*

30

356 FRONT STREET

ONLY HALF OF ANNE'S FACE was visible as she looked back at me, shadow covering the other half. A street lamp outside her office window was the strongest light in the mostly dark room; a tiny lamp added a spray of light in the far corner. We looked at each other as she rolled a few things over in her mind—or maybe a lot of things. Deep in thought, she looked to the side, where the window was. She got up, walked to the window and stood looking out. "Hmm," she said. "I wonder where it goes."

"Where what goes?" I asked.

"The fog."

I looked out the window. The fog had lifted. It was perfectly clear. "What time is it?" I asked.

"8:45," she answered, looking at her dainty wristwatch as she stood in the glow of the street lamp.

"Almost four hours. Not what you had in mind, I'm sure," I said.

"Well, that's true," she replied still looking out. "But it's alright."

"I suppose I better get going," I said as I stood up, looking at my phone for messages. There weren't any.

"I understand. When would you like to come back? Thursday evenings at this time would work. Or, I mean, 5 o'clock."

"Really?" I asked.

"Mm hmm. You wanted to come back, didn't you?"

"Well, I'd love to, but you had mentioned on the phone you weren't taking any new regular clients."

She smiled. "You'll be the exception, Jessica."

"Well, okay. Let me see. I'll call you when I know for sure."

"That's fine," she said starting toward the door. I walked in front of her.

"About my panic attacks," I said as I turned. "Anything I should do between now and the next time I see you? You see, the truth is, the wedding is in six weeks, and I was just hoping you could give me something, anything, to help me get through the anxiety I have been feeling. Techniques of some sort. Exercises, that kind of thing."

"Hmm," she said. "I didn't realize that's what you wanted."

"Oh, okay. Well, maybe next time."

"Well, look," she offered. "You've built a life on the value of doing. What you were doing was trying to be perfect for your dad, trying to please your husband, trying to find love with all those men. Now you're going to have to build a life on the value of being. And as far as I can tell, Joe is the only man you never had to perform for."

I looked her in the eye. "I hadn't thought about that."

"Well, just think about it. We'll talk about it next time."

We walked through her small waiting area and to the door at the far end. I opened it and stepped out. "I'm sorry I went so over."

"Not at all," she said, looking rather exhausted in the new light of the nearby walkway lamp.

Before turning to walk to my car, I offered her my hand. "I'll think about what you said; I really will. Thank you so much."

"That's good," she said. "See you next time."

I walked to my car in the clear night air, opened the door and sat inside. I turned the ignition and began to back out of the parking space. The anxiety I had been feeling suddenly felt a lot like excitement.

31
WHEN GRAVITY
WENT MISSING

THE FLOWERS BLOOMED that morning, the breeze rustled in the trees, the waves crashed against the rocks, and the world seemed that it was as it should be, except for one thing. Gravity seemed to be missing, at least for me. I had five consecutive weeks of Anne's care and wise counsel and over that time had felt my heart fill with joy at the prospect of healing. I knew I was on the road to being emotionally whole, and I was marrying the most patient man in the world, which meant that I could take my time and slowly find my way through the fog of my past. And now, I could barely contain my joy. I was floating along like a dandelion in the breeze.

I was with my bridesmaids laughing and giggling in the pristinely white bridal dressing room with a shock of blue from the Pacific Ocean visible in the windows. The girls were giving the photographer a little bit of flirty frustration has he tried to wrangle us into candid, pensive photos. There was too much joy in the room for anything remotely that serious. Suddenly I had the idea of the century.

"Here's what I want you to do," I grabbed and told Lyndi, looking stunning in her rose, chiffon dress. "I want you to run across the way and tell Joe that I love him and I can't wait to be married to him, okay?"

"Okay!" she whispered as if she just heard the greatest secret ever.

"Okay, go!" I said.

Just then there was a knock at the door. It was the director from the wedding venue. My mom spoke to him. "Jessica, honey" mom said as she closed the door.

"Yes!" I said happily.

"Well, the director says the stoves are broken and the company who fixes them won't be here till next week."

"Uh oh," Melanie, one of my bridesmaids said. "That means the food's going to be cold?"

"Well, maybe not, they're working the problem and they've got some options. They just wanted to let us know. I guess I should have just kept it to myself until I knew for sure if they couldn't remedy the problem."

"Don't worry," Melanie said to me with sympathy. "I'm sure they'll think of something."

"Yeah, honey," Ricki, my dear friend from the YMCA said. "They're just being upfront with you, but they'll find a way."

I walked toward them with a sullen face. "Cold food?" I said deep in thought. "A wedding party with cold food?"

"Well, maybe not," my mom said with a bit of urgency. "Let's just wait and see."

I sat in the chair, and they all came around me. "Here's my answer to that," I said. "I'm getting married! Who cares!"

I stood and twirled in my white-as-snow dress as the girls all laughed, and I sat down in a happy crash in front of the mirror again. "Ida, would you mind giving my hair a look over one more time just for the freaking fun of it?"

"Not at all!" Irma, from the support group, said with as much excitement as I could have ever hoped for. It was such a gift to have all our hair done by someone who had been through so much pain. Now here she was giving her talent away to my entire bridal party and smiling from ear to ear.

"I think it looks great!" she said.

"Me, too," I yelped. "But let's fix it some more!"

Just then Lyndi came back from across the way. "I have a message for you from Joe!" she said.

"What is it?"

"He says, 'I love you, too!'"

"Whoohoo!" all my bridesmaids shouted.

"I'm getting married to that beautiful man!" I screamed.

Under warm San Diego skies, mom and Sam met me at the top of the aisle, ready to walk me down and give me away. At the end of the aisle stood Joe alongside his best man, Rory, 12 years old, looking handsome and the picture of joy. I don't think I could have ever let myself imagine something like this could happen to me. Everything in my past seemed to have been a stepping-stone that led me here to these people, to this moment.

As I walked to the Wedding March, it seemed like I'd been plucked from another world and placed on the white satin that lined the aisle and pointed the way to the altar. The birds were singing, and I could hear the waves clapping along from just over the bluff. So much beauty. So much peace. In Joe's eyes were a mixture of love for me and for the God who had spoken so loudly and clearly in his life. As I passed the rows of faces, it was as holy a moment as I had yet experienced. Friends from church were in attendance, women from the ministry who knew my story were there praying for each step I took. Anne was there smiling her support. Family from the east coast, work friends, my mom's friends, Joe's friends and family made up the audience. The girl who was once isolated from the world now had so many loving faces to look at. The thought went through my mind, *I guess God wins in the end.* And He certainly did. Without Him, this never would have been the remotest of possibilities.

"I promise to wake up every day with the intention of making you happy," Joe said as he spoke the vows he wrote for me while holding my hands. "I promise to be the husband and father that you and Rory deserve. I promise to be a spiritual leader, holding us accountable and encouraging us to be a Godly example of marriage to others..."

I shook my head ever so slightly as he spoke, a small, I-can-hardly-believe-it smile on my face. He was so beautiful I couldn't wait another moment to be his. When he was done, I said to the pastor without taking my eyes off Joe, "Is it okay if I kiss him now?"

About 15 minutes later, the vows had been made, candles had been lit, rings had been exchanged, a short sermon had been given and it was time for the pastor to make his pronouncement. We turned toward the audience. "I now pronounce you husband and wife," the pastor said. "You may now kiss your husband."

The normally extremely public-affection-shy Joe stepped up to the occasion and laid one on me, matching my enthusiasm lip for lip. At that moment it went through my mind that a kiss and a prayer were not so different.

After the ceremony, Rory found some other kids to run around with on the grass, the Pacific Ocean in the background. I'm not sure I had ever seen him so light and free. The introduction of Joe into his life was as transforming a moment as could ever be—so much more than I could have ever dreamed. My boy seemed to be slated for such heartache and hardship, but no more. Joe had given Rory a new life.

The reception hall was filled with the brilliant sound of glasses tinkling, forks against plates, people talking and laughing, chairs being scooted back and forth, babies crying. It was a cacophony of celebration; the sound of merriment. I could hardly believe it was happening to me and for me. "I want to thank you for coming into my life and becoming my best friend," Rory said in his best-man speech, the microphone booming against his lips. "But what I'm most excited about is that you're not just a friend anymore. Now you're a part of my family."

Joe's younger brother Charles then took the mic and gave a heartfelt thanks to Joe for being the father figure in his life, as well as a role model who always steered him in the right direction. "And now I'd like to take a moment to pass Joe on to Rory so that he can have the opportunity that I had, to grow up with a wonderful man to admire and look up to."

Initially I wasn't sure that Rory would understand how beautiful the moment was, but when I saw the tears streaming down his face, I knew that I was wrong. Rory was getting his heart's desire. So was I.

32

LITTLE JESSICA

"**W**HAT WOULD YOU like to say to her," Anne said. "Close your eyes, hold her and tell her."

Anne felt that it would be profitable for me to go back in time and visit little Jessica and square some things away. I would sit in Anne's office with the shades drawn and visualize her with crazy strawberry hair going in every direction and large brown eyes that stared back at me with a little bit of bewilderment. I would pick her up and hold her to my chest and I would rock her. "You're beautiful just the way you are, Jess." I would say though tears. "You never had to do anything to be lovely enough to be loved, but I know you thought you did."

Anne also had me write her a letter. It was at once painful and beautiful.

Dear sweet Jessica,

I'm so sorry you had to endure what you did as a young girl. You were enough just as you were, perfect in all of your imperfection. Your feisty spirit and inquisitive personality were anything but a nuisance—in fact, you were marvelous. I'm sorry you didn't feel the unconditional love of your father and that you had to grow up longing for a closeness that would never come. As you grew older you deserved to be told you were beautiful, intelligent, courageous and kind. I'm sorry that your generous spirit was taken advantage of as your desire to feel loved and valued grew. I'm sorry that there was no one to protect you in your most desperate moments. I'm sorry I didn't have the tools to find fulfillment outside of what became a very destructive relationship. I believe your dad did the very best he could and loved you in every way he knew how. He would be so proud of you today. I'm certain of it.

Over time, however, I realized that Little Jessica responded to the holding of her body more than the affirming words. So there in Anne's office, I would close my eyes, take Jessica in my arms and simply hold her close. And she liked it.

So that is what I now do. The little girl who longed for love now gets it in full as she curls up in my arms and feels my heart beat for her. I am happy to report she is deeply satisfied.

EPILOGUE

I N 2011, 10 YEARS AFTER he was found guilty, Trent objected to the food in the mess hall of a prison in Oklahoma. The altercation erupted into a riot and in the chaos, he was repeatedly beaten over the head, suffering wounds that were consistent with being pummeled with a baseball bat. I received a phone call from his sister that he was on life-support. He had severe swelling to the brain, many crushed bones and the prognosis was bleak.

When I got the news, I was in my office at work. I burst into tears and was so distraught for so long, my supervisor sent me home. I was an absolute mess. My reaction surprised even me. I quickly had to make sense of why I felt so devastated.

My search for an answer led me down many paths. Was it the thought of such a funny, handsome and charismatic young man coming to a lonely demise as he lay handcuffed to a state hospital bed? Was it the thought of a sad end to a life that had experienced almost no happiness? Was it the thought of his family, who had already been through so much, having to endure the pain of burying their son and never saying goodbye? It was for all these reasons, but it was also something else.

The closer I got to the truth of what was really in my heart, the clearer I understood my grief. Even though Trent's release date was far away, 2025, I lived with fear of that date, as if my life of torment at the hands of Trent would somehow resume when he walked out of the prison gates. The truth I had to come to terms with was that I wanted him to die.

I fell into a panic that felt like it was laced with elation. I began to call the prison for updates multiple times a day, which drove them crazy. I thought about his death, I longed for his death, and I prayed for his death—then had to deal with all the guilt that went with it. I couldn't stop the collision of the two emotions, and I was reduced to tears many times throughout the day. I was so distracted, I was absolutely useless at work and why I wasn't fired, or even warned, is a mystery.

Time spent with Anne was critical. Initially, she thought my condition was a type of Stockholm Syndrome, where captives come to care deeply about their captors. It soon became clear that what might have appeared to be *care* was rather somebody struggling at their constraints—I simply had never felt truly free of Trent. For all the healing and conversion experiences and time spent in love with Joe, there was an inexplicable tether to Trent that kept me in bondage. It wasn't care or concern or love. It was that the fear he created in me was in the fabric of who I was. Once I got a clear view of it, I had a decision to make.

"Now, it's your time to choose," Anne said. "You can choose freedom, or you can choose bondage. Truth is, real freedom is never about anything on the outside of your body or mind, but on the inside. It has nothing to do with your circumstances, and it has nothing to do with Trent. It never has. Your joy and sanity and freedom are all in how you choose."

Up to that point, I was afraid to associate my name with my work in the ministry and didn't even want it to appear on the letterhead. I was even considering a different name as a way of adding a buffer of protection. It was crazy. I let Trent dominate me from behind prison walls, two thousand miles away. Finally I was ready to walk into the light of the life I chose and not one that he did.

Today, I am resolved that if it is my time to go, it is my time to go. I have to keep in mind that I could have died a thousand times over at the hands of Trent, and God never let that happen. So I walk unafraid. My name is proudly on the cover of this book and on everything I do. I am safe and set free and I have no fear. I have made that choice.

To the best of my knowledge,
Trent made a full recovery from his injuries.
He is still scheduled for release in August of 2025.

Rory has grown up to be a kind, generous, sensitive, and very well-adjusted young man and is proud to identify as African-American.

ACKNOWLEDGMENTS

I'D LIKE TO TAKE THE opportunity to thank my mother for her steadfast belief in me, undying love and support, and for teaching me what it means to be a woman of service. Special thanks to my brother for the hours of work he put into this project as editor and mentor, his words of encouragement, and belief in my purpose. My husband for guiding me into the arms of my Savior, for loving me before I loved myself, and being my biggest fan. My son for his generous, kind, caring, and fun-loving spirit that he blesses me with every day. My closest friends (you know who you are) for lifting me up when I've doubted myself, pushing me forward in love, and confirming my worth in Him. To the Garcia, McGuire, and Shapiro families for their remarkably generous contributions to this book, and to the many others who have given in order to make this happen.

Thanks, too, to Jonathan Smith and BlueFair Photography for great photos, Nancy Lair, Sheerah Haywood for their careful editorial eye on different versions of the manuscript, Ben Monson for his brilliant cover design, 1106 Design for their exceptional work in creating the layout, and my outstanding, go-to printer and distributor, Lightening Source.

Special thanks to my publicist and friend, Melanie Figaro, for believing in this movement, not being afraid to push the envelope, creating strategies and identifying opportunities that only she could, and ultimately, being the driving force behind what has become nosilencenoviolence.org.

And last, but certainly not least, my co-author, Dave Franco. Without you, this book would not be. For the endless hours of discussion, the multiple revisions, your eagerness to represent my truth, belief in my story, putting words and meaning to periods of my life that had no words, and for creating a masterpiece that has the capacity to change millions of lives around the world.

In seven years, more than six thousand women, men and children have been through the ministry that is today called, H.E.A.L.I.N.G. It has inspired additional H.E.A.L.I.N.G. ministries in Michigan, New York and Los Angeles. If you would like to donate to H.E.A.L.I.N.G., or start a H.E.A.L.I.N.G. ministry in your community, please log onto www.jessicayaffa.org to download guidelines.

CPSIA information can be obtained at www.ICGtesting.com
Printed in the USA
BVOW02s1226100414

350223BV00003B/72/P